THE ACTOR IN TRAINING

THE ACTOR
IN TRAINING

By

MORRIS FISHMAN
L.R.A.M. (Speech and Drama)
Diploma in Dramatic Art (London University)

GREENWOOD PRESS, PUBLISHERS
WESTPORT, CONNECTICUT

Library of Congress Cataloging in Publication Data

Fishman, Morris.
   The actor in training.

   Reprint of the ed. published by H. Jenkins, London.
   Bibliography: p.
   1. Acting--Study and teaching. I. Title.
[PN2075.F5 1974]   792'.028   73-11748
ISBN 0-8371-7087-7

PN
2075
F5
1974

First published in 1961 by Herbert Jenkins, London

Reprinted with the permission of Barrie & Jenkins

Reprinted in 1974 by Greenwood Press,
a division of Williamhouse-Regency Inc.

Library of Congress Catalog Card Number 73-11748

ISBN 0-8371-7087-7

Printed in the United States of America

FOREWORD

Mr. Fishman's book can be of the greatest help to the English theatre—if aspiring actors and actresses can take its lucid teaching to heart. Our theatre suffers—among others—two particular ills. The first is an idea that acting is easy, and in consequence amateur acting, which for thousands of people constitutes their only experience of the art, is permanently at a low level of achievement. The second is the lack of any knowledge about acting in the minds of that part of the public which still supports the professional theatre.

This absence of any idea in the public mind of "what makes an actor tick" is a serious matter to those who care about the theatre. Curiosity is man's peculiar and especial attribute, but unfortunately curiosity about theatre-technique is as a rule only of a kind such as is satisfied by the reminiscences of stars and Sunday gossip writers.

Mr. Fishman's book will, I hope, stimulate curiosity of a different kind. The power of any art to stimulate the mind as well as to please the senses springs from a duality inherent in all art—the balance between technique and inspiration, form and content, the 'how' and the 'what'.

It is the especial merit of "The Actor in Training" that it shows, directly and simply, just why the 'how' and the 'what' comprise an artistic whole: moreoever, in its very clear explanations of how the ground work of truth in acting can be achieved, it leaves no doubt that hard work and hard thinking are as essential to actors as imagination—the artist needs both.

All those who intend to take up a theatrical career should read this book—*before* they start their initial training at a drama school.

John Fernald

INTRODUCTION

This book aims to help the teacher of Acting and his pupil—the novice who aspires to become proficient in the most elusive of arts. In it no distinction is made between the amateur and professional but only between the good and bad actor.

The experiments and exercises described in the following pages were tried out while I was resident instructor in Acting and Play Production in a Theatre Training School in Birmingham. For two years I was in the enviable position of having carte blanche to plan my own course and to train actors and actresses for a theatre, which although of amateur status, had achieved a high level of performance. The students under my care were later to take their place in a live theatre company and not to be fettered by the fear of unemployment in the hazardous world of the professional theatre. Like their fellows in the professional theatre school where I later taught, some were young enough to believe that they knew all there was to know, and others old enough to share the instructor's view that there was still much to learn. The number of students in the class was usually between twelve and fifteen and they attended for two evening periods of two hours per week. The first period was usually devoted to Movement and Voice Production, and the second to Acting Technique, in which integration of the various facets of acting was attempted. All students had been graded as a result of an initial interview and audition. Their ages ranged from seventeen to fifty. The number attending each class and the wide range of ability proved ideal for my purpose.

The main body of the book contains descriptions of experiments. Their intention is:

1. to devise a series of imaginative exercises for the training of the actor and actress, and to test their efficacy with a wide range of students;
2. to observe common errors in Acting Technique and to attempt to find effective remedies for them;
3. to integrate exercises which have proved successful into a general course of instruction in the technique of acting. The comprehensive type of course described in the Appendix will, it is hoped, prove to be of assistance to drama teachers in the planning of the syllabus.

Supplementary exercises have then been added so that the instructor has a fund of material at his disposal. These exercises follow the same lines as the experiments and many of them are extracts from well-known plays, copies of which are easily obtainable.

Much of the material employed is derived from games and exercises in current use. Most of it is based on my own experience as an actor and producer in the amateur and professional theatres.

The two preliminary chapters on the "Schools of Acting" and the "General Requirements of the Actor" are intended to serve as an introduction to the practical work.

CONTENTS

ACKNOWLEDGMENTS

I am indebted to the following for kindly allowing me to reproduce material:—

Mr. Noel Coward and Messrs. Curtis Brown for the extract from *Still Life*; Mr. John Osborne and Messrs. Faber and Faber for the passage from *Look Back in Anger*; Miss Athene Seyler and Messrs. J. Garnet Miller for the extract from *The Craft of Comedy*; Sir Michael Redgrave and Messrs. William Heinemann for the quotation from *The Actor's Ways and Means*; Messrs. Longmans, Green & Company for the diagram of The Resonator Scale, which is adapted from the original in *The Voice*, by W. A. Aiken, M.D.; Messrs. George Allen and Unwin for the extract from Dr. Gilbert Murray's translation of the *Alcestis* of Euripides; Messrs. Geoffrey Bles for the passage from *An Actor Prepares*, by Constantin Stanislavsky.

I am also grateful to E. J. Burton, M.A. for his assistance in the initial stages of preparation and to M. Screech, D.Litt. for his kindly help and advice throughout. Moreover I am greatly indebted to Mr. John Fernald for consenting to write the Foreword.

M.F.

THE ACTOR IN TRAINING

★ I ★

The Schools of Acting

THE art of acting is essentially concerned with action, not theory. Consequently this book is primarily concerned with practice. However a certain amount of background information must be given in order that the motives underlying the practical exercises may be understood by actor and instructor. It is for this reason that I begin by describing systems and styles of acting advocated by some of its foremost exponents—each of them a worker in theatre. None wrote from the remoteness of his study without personal experience to support his beliefs. All held the opinion that theory helps practice and practice helps theory.

The actor's art is creative just as the musician's art is creative. The musician uses an instrument to convey the composer's work to the listener; the actor uses his own body for exactly the same purpose—to convey the playwright's words and thoughts to an audience. He is therefore performer and instrument all in one. The first must be proficient and the second tuned up and ready to fulfil its purpose. It is the object of theatrical training to help achieve this.

Methods of training actors are usually very closely related to specific styles of acting. In some instances a particular theatre, by virtue of the tradition it has established, sets the standard, and its stamp is felt in many Drama Academies. Such is the case of the Comédie Française with its own school, and others run on similar

15

lines. Sometimes influences stem from far afield. One has only to think of the influence on the Group Theatre in New York of the Moscow Art Theatre, culminating in the much popularised "Method". Occasionally individual performers help to evolve a personal style which students learn to imitate. It is certain that in this country Shakespearian acting owes much to Sir John Gielgud and to Sir Laurence Olivier. Their styles of acting influence our Drama Schools in no small measure.

It is relevant therefore to examine the various systems of training while relating them to the particular styles of acting from which they are derived and whose patterns they attempt to follow. These styles or schools of acting may be broadly classified into two main groups:

1. those who place the main emphasis on the development of the actor's *external technique*, that is, his speech, movement and gesture; and
2. those who think it is more important to foster the growth of his *internal technique*, that is, his thoughts, feelings and emotions.

THE REPRESENTATIONAL SCHOOL OF ACTING

The best exponents of this style are the artists of the Comédie Française and its chief propagandist is Coquelin, the author of *The Art of the Actor*, who asserts quite categorically that the actor in performance should not himself experience the emotions he is attempting to portray. "Art", he says, "is not identification but representation." He adds, "The famous axiom. 'If thou wouldst make me weep, weep then thyself', is not therefore applicable to the actor." According to Diderot, the great French theoretician of the eighteenth century, the 'paradox' of the actor lay in the fact that to move others, he must remain cold and unmoved himself. In the preliminary rehearsals he might allow himself the luxury of emotion, but once its outward pattern had been fixed, he must discipline himself to remain calm and to give the same performance night after night. At the height of his passion he should be sufficiently cool and collected to ask for a cup of coffee. Thus the training of actors of this school consists of indoctrinating them with an abundance of external technique—the gymnastics of the art. Suppleness of voice and movement are its precepts, and finesse and economy of Style (with a capital "S"), its results in practice. The finished product is a consummate technician with an efficient instrument at his command upon which he can play. Very little is said about that inner man whose feelings, thoughts and emotions are to infuse this instrument with life, except that "he must not experience a shadow of the sentiments he is expressing—at the very moment when he is expressing them with the greatest truthfulness and power."

For many of the plays of Molière, Racine and Corneille this style of acting with its attendant system of training has proved itself successful. Racine in particular constructed his works to a formal pattern based on Greek Tragedy, exploiting a verse metre alien to our ears, the rhyming Alexandrine couplet. The Alexandrine demands a set inflection to bring out the meaning and emphasis of a line, and for a long time the teaching of "the only correct intonation" (la seule inflection juste) was part of the training at the Conservatoire de Musique et de Déclamation. Again, the comedies of Molière are performed with traditional business, demanding sleight of hand and timing of a very high order as well as impeccable articulation. Comedy playing certainly requires a great deal of faultless external technique. More will be said later on this subject.

As far as the Representational School of Acting is concerned one can commend it for the stress it places on the training of the actor's instrument, while realising its deficiencies as far as training and developing his imagination, that other essential to his art. It is doubtful whether these methods of total inner calm would succeed if applied to the works of Chekhov, Arthur Miller or

2

Tennessee Williams. They certainly fail if employed by the actor preparing to take part in one of Shakespeare's masterpieces. The audience will detect that lack of heart which the most mellifluous voice, the most graceful movements, cannot hide.

THE VOCAL SCHOOL

It has for long been realised that in the training of the actor, the role of voice production is of paramount importance. So much so that many have made it the cornerstone of their system, to the exclusion of all else. With them the voice beautiful and expressive is everything. They believe, with the Representationalists, that the actor's instrument is all important, but part company with them on the issue of training the rest of the instrument as thoroughly as the vocal part.

There are several excellent systems of Speech Training and it is not proposed to describe any of them here, particularly as the subject is dealt with in more detail in Chapter Thirteen. Excellent work is done by our Dramatic Schools and it is not my intention to deprecate their methods. It is only when Speech Training is not adequately supplemented by the other essentials that it can prove to be harmful. The voice is one of the fundamentals in projecting the performance, but to make it the be all and end all is fatal to the artist, who needs to develop the inner powers of creation which help him to say something *imaginatively*, otherwise the interpretation of the author's text is always on the surface level, and the disembodied voice is the result, carefully modulated, impeccably articulated and expressing—nothing. Many teachers of elocution are turning out such voice-conscious aspirants to the stage who are often nothing more than the reciters of party pieces. As a producer of plays I have suffered much at the hands of people who have been bound by the system in its pure, unadultered form.

THE SCHOOL OF PURE MOVEMENT AND MIME

Dance Drama, Movement, Ballet and Mime—every one can help the actor. After all they are just as much theatrical representations as the performance of the straight play. Unfortunately the artist can all too easily be trained in such a way that his proficiency in these elements predominates at the expense of others of equal importance. Balletic movements and formal mime then take the place of natural (or seemingly natural) walking and handling of properties, and are not part of that art which should conceal art. Such actors float across the stage or take up the fifth position on the flimsiest excuse. The art of histrionic interpretation may have begun with mime: before the word the action. With them however it stops there. When the word is added, it is often so feeble that one is forced to conclude that this method, although ideal for ballet training, requires something more to supplement it.

THE RUBBER STAMP SYSTEM

Another method which has been in the fashion for some years now is what is called, for want of a better name, the Rubber Stamp system. It can be briefly described thus: the teacher has at his disposal a series of stock situations, such as quarrels, love scenes, accusations or denunciations, which he has compiled from a large variety of plays, ancient and modern. He rehearses his pupils in these scenes until some measure of proficiency is achieved. The scenes are now considered blueprints or model answers for similar situations as they arise in other plays. All the tricks which might have been effective in the rehearsal and subsequent performance of the quarrel scene in say *Julius Caesar* are to be used again in the famous second act of Noel Coward's *Private Lives*. Exits and entrances follow a certain routine, love scenes are played in a minor key, tragic scenes must be played in the manner of "To be or not to be." Gradually the student builds up a store of rubber stamp originals, which are to be used again, when the new situation has been identified and classified as suitable for this or that treatment.

Now every teacher of acting technique has to compile a series of exercises which his students must religiously carry out. Breathing exercises, voice placing exercises, movement routines—these are but a few of those which the tyro must practise. These however are only an aid to freeing the body of those tensions and physical obstacles which impede it from expressing and re-creating the dramatist's intention. Again, extracts from plays are often used by the finest teachers in order to help their students to come to grips with the problems which will beset them when they tackle complete roles in full length plays; in such cases however, the extract is material for the students' creative work—it is not a repetition of last week's treatment of a similar scene. The teacher will not say "Remember how good you were as 'Jones' last week?—Well do the same with this part—the situations are similar—play it the same way, and use some of the business we found so effective." Instead he will prompt the student to bring his faculties into play to create something new. The good actor does not copy blindly, just as he does not repeat his words parrot fashion.

Why is the Rubber Stamp system so harmful? Because it teaches the actor to take the easy way of repeating set tricks, soon recognisable by the audience as personal mannerisms of the performer, without relevance to the meaning and content of the play. Because it has nothing to do with that re-creative art which is part of the actor's task. Because it is counterfeit and absolves the actor from doing the necessary preparatory work on his role. Lastly, because it is responsible for the one-performance man who is as immutable and unchanging as a block of granite.

STANISLAVSKY AND THE "METHOD"

The next school of acting to come under review, and one which deserves the most serious attention, is that based on the

"Stanislavsky" system. This great Russian actor and director evolved a method which has had far reaching results on both his contemporaries and on theatrical workers of other lands, notably the United States, where in the "Actors' Studio" of Lee Strasberg and in the Film and Theatre work of Elia Kazan many successes have been achieved. In this country much of the work of so outstanding a teacher and director as Michel St. Denis, both in his London Theatre Studio and at the Old Vic Theatre School, was to some extent influenced by it. Today the "Method", as it is reverently called by its advocates, is much under discussion in theatrical circles. It has found many derisive opponents as well as many fanatical supporters. Both factions often confuse the real issue. In any case Stanislavsky himself did not want his observations to be considered unalterable laws of grammar to be strictly adhered to by disciples learning a stock theatrical language, for he was continually experimenting and making new discoveries. He preferred to work in the theatre rather than be one of its pontiffs.

The Stanislavsky system attempts to help the actor discover that creative mood in which he can give of his best. This it does by physical means and by exercises which give practice in the development of imagination and creative fantasy, the understanding of the clues to performance offered by the playwright, the development of concentration and freedom from excessive muscular constriction, the discovery of the core or main purpose of the role and its place in theme of the play. These exercises help the actor to identify himself with his part. By their aid the author's intention can be more effectively interpreted and subquently translated into action. This is but a short list of the many things which go to make up the system. It will be noticed that so far they are concerned with what is called the Inner or Internal Technique. In his autobiography *My Life in Art* Stanislavsky tells how by rigorous self-examination and constant research he eventually made these discoveries. It is a wonderful book, written by an artist full of humility in the face of the Herculean task which he had set himself as his life's work. Later, he set down his conclusions in more systematic form in his much discussed book *An Actor Prepares:* the main part of this volume, which is written in the form of a series of discussion between a wise and experienced teacher and his pupils, deals with this inner technique.

Misinterpreters of the system often quote *An Actor Prepares* as their Bible and are apt to use the terms employed in it as a kind of Open Sesame to the art of acting. It will be seen later that concepts such as "emotion memory" and "creative fantasy" can help the student to perform sincerely in a small room—once the terms are really understood and put into practice. The student often forgets however that they are of little assistance to him in projecting or enlarging his performance to reach the more distant rows of a public theatre. Stanislavsky himself understood this, because in his subsequent book, *Building a Character*, he deals in great detail with movement, diction, singing, intonation and pauses, and making the body expressive. Much of this then is concerned with *external* technique, although quite rightly Stanislavsky never treats this in isolation, as something to be grafted on to the other part of the method. The fact is that *Building a Character* was published at a much later date than *An Actor Prepares*, and consequently the first part of the system was swallowed by many without the necessary corrective contained in the second volume. Many amateurs who substitute talking about the part for trying it out in practice owe many of their misconceptions to a half digested reading of *An Actor Prepares* and a total ignorance of *Building a Character*. According to them Voice Training and Movement Practice are dangerous because they might lead to loss of sincerity and to 'getting out of the skin of their parts.' They speak of 'feeling right' and 'being sincere' but squeeze emotion out of themselves in such a way as to destroy theatrical illusion. This is the very thing that Stanislavsky himself deplored.

THE 'METHOD'

Today one hears of the 'Method'. In America the writings of Stanislavsky bore fruit in the mode of rehearsal and production practised by the 'Group Theatre' of Harold Clurman, Lee Strasberg and Elia Kazan in those chaotic days of the 1930's. New playwrights wrote for them, notably Clifford Odets, and when the Group dissolved in 1941 their work was recognised as being of a high order. A fascinating account of the rise and subsequent fall of this fine theatre ensemble is given by Harold Clurman in his book *The Fervent Years*. Its methods have been resuscitated in the Actors' Studio which is run by Lee Strasberg and Elia Kazan. Here actors and actresses, many with established reputations, go to give performances of extracts and improvisations which are subsequently criticised and discussed by Mr. Strasberg and an audience of actors and students. This must be an ordeal for the performer, but as it is self-imposed one imagines that he believes he is deriving some benefit from it. It must be realised however that the most creative work with the actor in preparation of his role is often done in private rehearsal with the minimum of bystanders, and that such public criticism is abhorred by both actor and producer. There can be no doubt that Strasberg is a brilliant teacher and a sincere artist who is dedicated to the theatre. He has gathered round him disciples who, when they rise to theatrical heights, publicly assert that it is due to the fact that they are "Studio" trained. Such are Marlon Brando, Julie Harris and Eli Wallach; they are sometimes called "Method Actors".

Accounts given by those who have witnessed the 'Method' in action describe how Strasberg analyses performances according to their psychological content and their theatrical effectiveness, mainly along the lines of the Stanislavsky system. There are many opponents. Some say that this psychological analysis goes too far and has built up a highfalutin' jargon of its own. Others, with more reason, contend that the lack of attention given to diction and voice projection does not sufficiently equip the student to do full justice to difficult passages of Shakespeare, Shaw or Christopher Fry, in which the powers and efficacy of the human vocal instrument are stretched to its limits. This defect is being remedied and regular instruction is now being given by qualified teachers.

One cannot leave this all too brief reference to the Stanislavsky system without describing some of the pitfalls and difficulties which beset those who attempt to put it into practice. First, it requires a group or artists working together over a considerable period of time; that is virtually impossible in this country under present conditions. One has only to read Mr. Richard Findlater's *Unholy Trade* to realise how fluid and unstable these conditions really are. The second point, which has already been hinted at, is the danger of having only a passing knowledge of the method, for this can lead the beginner into a morass of technical jargon, pseudo-psychology and a type of intellectual acting which deprives the audience of the real magic of the theatre—the living performance which moves those who are privileged to witness it. Then, if the actor is not careful, he will tend to neglect that important instrument of external technique, the human voice, and will be inclined to squeeze emotion out of himself under the impression that he is being sincere. We need another Group Theatre, a London Theatre Studio, or another Old Vic Theatre School, where conditions obtain which are favourable to its success. However all this is mere cavilling. Up to the present this has proved to be the most effective system of training the actor. Its chief virtue lies in the fact that it is an integrated system which does not depend on the dissection of the human frame and the intellectual and emotional machine into component parts without reforming them as a synthetic whole. One other thing is certain: it is a good springboard for further research.

BERTOLT BRECHT AND THE ESTRANGEMENT OF THE AUDIENCE

In direct opposition to the theories of Stanislavsky can be placed those of the German poet, playwright, theatrical director and revolutionary, Bertolt Brecht. Whereas Stanislavsky states that the actor must identify himself with his role, Brecht asserts that he must on the contrary act as a reporter of the action. On no account must the audience be allowed to become involved in the action of the play—they must be made to *think*, be prompted to *make decisions*. The actor is a mixture of lecturer, commentator and reporter.

Now all this seems like madness to those who have been reared in the naturalistic tradition of acting, where the audience must be made to forget that it is in a theatre; but Brecht's plays were not naturalistic. He evolved what he called the Epic Theatre, and his plays were supposed to contain scenes devoid of climax and pathetic overtones, atmosphere and mood; these, he contended, merely lull the spectator into a false sense of believing that he is involved in the thick of the action. No, the audience must be made to think and in order to do that it must be "estranged" from the action of the scene, that is, it must not be emotionally identified with the characters of the play. The staging of his plays is not naturalistic—actors may wear masks, songs are introduced, titles are displayed on posters flown from the wings, and other devices are employed to illustrate the argument of the playwright. Narrators are also used to interrupt the play. Those who wish to know more about his theories should read his treatise *The Little Organum of the Theatre*.

One wonders whether it is the audience rather than the actor that requires training for this type of theatre. I have myself produced Brecht's play *The Good Woman of Setzuan* with a stylised setting and found that the audience were quite moved in those scenes which did lend themselves to audience-involvement. Later, I saw Brecht's production of his own play *The Caucasian*

Chalk Circle and was much moved by many of its sequences. The effect of estrangement was evoked by the setting and scenery rather than by the acting, and the only time that the actors seemed to be reporters or commentators was when they sang a type of choral interlude akin to that of the chorus in a Shakespearean History, commenting on the progress of the story. In the main body of the play the actors appeared to be completely identified with their roles. Here theory and practice seemed to differ.

It is doubtful whether all this can really help the Actor in training. The actor is often a reporter of the action of the play, and sometimes quite directly so, as in the Shakespearean prologues or to take a modern example, the Stage Manager in Thornton Wilder's *Our Town*. Here too he must establish direct contact with an audience, must speak to it and produce a calculated effect—but that effect is certainly not to estrange them from the action. In *Richard III* the initial soliloquy begins

> Now is the winter of our discontent
> Made glorious summer by this sun of York:
> And all the clouds that lour'd upon our house
> In the deep bosom of the ocean buried.
> Now are our brows bound with victorious wreaths;
> Our bruised arms hung up for monuments;
> Our stern alarums changed to merry meetings;
> Our dreadful marches to delightful measures.

This sets the mood of the play for the audiences and indicates what is to happen soon after. So do the introductory speeches to the audience in *Our Town* and in Tennessee Williams *Glass Menagerie*. Both help the spectator to suspend his disbelief and to put himself in a state of receptiveness. It is in the 'aside' of the Comedy of Manners that the performer comes nearest to the envisaged Brechtian type of actor and must keep a cool heart. Brecht's actor must in fact be one of those trained according to the precepts of Diderot and Coquelin, though not on this occasion in order to move people but to make them think, to take decisions, to act so as to change the world. Unfortunately Brecht himself says very little on how this actor is to be trained.

OTHER INFLUENCES

This account of the various schools and their related styles is necessarily incomplete. For instance Meyerhold and his 'bio-mechanics'—in direct opposition to his former teacher, Stanis-lavsky—can only be cursorily mentioned as the initiator of an acrobatic form of training with an emphasis on 'hokum' or stage business. Copeau of the 'Vieux Colombier', Dullin, each had his influence in his day, but I can do little more than mention them here. In any case it is proposed to deal only with those aspects of training which are relevant to our purpose—the discovery of methods which might be of use in the training of the pupil actor, and much that these pioneers have offered has already been mentioned in the discussion of the other systems. Meanwhile one or two movements are bound to have an influence on the theatre of the future and consequently on the schooling of its artists. Such are Theatre in the Round and Child Drama.

In the first of these the performer is not confined to the picture-frame type of stage. There are a large number of prominent workers in the theatre who think that the picture frame stage has outlived its purpose and that theatres should be constructed and plays written which allow the audience to be closer to the action. Indeed the Questors, Ealing, houses an adjustable stage, which can readily be converted to a shape and size suitable to the specific type of play to be performed. Tyrone Guthrie's production of *The Three Estates* at the Edinburgh Festival was an example of successful Arena staging. These experiments are bound to affect methods of training. In Theatre in the Round the actor, being surrounded by his audience, must find new means of projection. He might have constantly to change his position to give all sections of the theatre their fair share of the action. Much depends on the size of the auditorium. If it is small the actor and the audience can achieve a degree of participation unheard of in the picture-frame theatre.

Finally, there are the experiments which are being carried out in the field of Child Drama. Here acting is a type of therapy, in which children can "play out" those instinctive urges which are at the root of anti-social behaviour, and so get them out of their system. The discoveries made by workers in this sphere may be of interest and assistance to those who wish to use every available source of information to help them in the formidable task of assisting the Actor in Training.

SUMMARY

Methods of training actors depend on specific styles of schools of acting. Some of these are:—

1. The Representational School—who believe that to move others the performer must himself remain unmoved.

2. The Vocal School—whose purpose is to train only the artist's voice and who forget that other parts of the human instrument need to be given attention.

3. The School of Pure Movement and Mime—with its excessive emphasis on these aspects of training.

4. The Rubber Stamp System. Here the teacher gives model answers which serve as rubber stamps to be used as the occasion demands. The actor is absolved of thinking for himself.

5. The Stanislavsky System which is based on a lifetime's research by a great Russian producer. It helps the student actor to identify himself with the role.

6. Bertolt Brecht and his estrangement effect. He believed that the actor should be a reporter or commentator and

not identified with his part. By this means the audience is to be 'estranged', or 'alienated' that is, prevented from becoming involved in the play.

7. Theatre in the Round—breaks away from the picture frame type of stage and can make for greater audience participation.

8. Child Drama in which the idea of 'playing out' anti-social urges can help to prevent delinquency. Its methods may be of use to the Drama Instructor.

General Requirements of the Actor

In the previous chapter it was seen how different teachers make widely different demands on their actor. One wants him to move the spectator while remaining unmoved himself. Another asks him to become identified with the role, while yet a third stipulates that he act as a reporter. All have this in common: they are stating their view of the actor's relationship with his audience.

There are some people who will never be made into proficient actors, however skilled and arduous the training to which subject themselves. This is because they cannot make contact with an audience; their effect on it is entirely negative. They are in the minority, however, and very few of them have any aspirations to theatrical fame. Most people can achieve a fair measure of success if they are really determined to take the trouble. Only great actors are born. Others can be made, but not overnight.

Sir Michael Redgrave in his stimulating book, *The Actor's Ways and Means*, says:

"The basis of all acting is undoubtedly instinctive, but that does not mean that a good deal of this is not susceptible to some kind of analysis, or that method may not make more than it mars."

The human instrument which is the actor's equipment has already been subjected to some sort of analysis by the statement that the schools of acting placed their emphasis on External

30

Technique or on Inner Technique. The time has come for this to be elaborated.

EXTERNAL EQUIPMENT

The external equipment of the actor consists of his voice, movement and gestures. These must be so organised to achieve the maximum effect on the audience for the minimum of effort on his part. This is the essence of good timing.

VOICE

The voice is the most important part of the external equipment. It must be clear, resonant and expressive, particularly for some of the heavier parts. Consider this passage from *Henry V*, Act II—

> Now all the youth of England are on fire,
> And silken dalliance in the wardrobe lies;
> Now thrive the armourers, and honour's thought
> Reigns solely in the breast of every man:
> They sell the pasture now to buy the horse,
> Following the mirror of all Christian Kings
> With winged heels, as English Mercuries.

It is difficult to imagine such lines spoken in a flat expressionless voice, and yet it takes a good deal of training to achieve the necessary control of the breath and tone to give them their full value. Passages in modern plays. even if they contain chatty, so-called naturalistic dialogue, must be heard. The influence of the film and the muttering, stuttering technique of some stars has encouraged others to do the same on the stage with unfortunate results. On the other hand not everything requires to be stressed, and beginners are apt to emphasise too many words, thereby emphasising nothing. Yet the exaggerated faith of some performers in throw-away mannerisms often makes one wish to shout out, 'Speak up'.

Not all of us are born with a good speaking voice. It can be acquired. Without it the student will never achieve success.

Having a good voice is in itself not enough. One must use it to speak the playwright's words as though they were one's own. Sensitivity to speech patterns, the ability to use pace, pitch and emphasis to 'ring the changes' are prime necessities. More on this subject will be given in the chapter on Speech Training.

MOVEMENT

Moving well is a prime necessity for stage work. That does not mean that all movements must be pretty and full of artificial grace. That depends on the play. Those of the eighteenth century, such as Sheridan's *School for Scandal*, demand a grace and artifice of movement in accordance with the manners of that age. In the seventeenth century comedy by Wycherley, *The Way of the World*, Millamant's entrance is described thus:

Here she comes in full sail . . .

The actress playing the part would look ludicrous if she strutted on to the stage in the modern teen-age manner.

On the other hand, Hester Collyer's first movement across the stage in Terence Rattigan's *The Deep Blue Sea* is the tired walk of a person for whom life has little left to offer.

By good movement is meant activity which is under the actor's control, movement which is relaxed and free from those constrictions and muscular tensions which beset us because of stage fright. Few performers are free of 'nerves', particularly on first nights, but the good actor uses these to give his performance 'body' and life. The beginner stiffens his muscles, constricts his throat, clenches his fists and thereby paralyses himself and dams up all the channels along which the performance must flow to reach the audience. People are often told 'to relax' in real life when they are under emotional or nervous strain. It is an irritating piece of advice to receive because it is easier said than done. Relaxation is a state of mind as well as a state of body and the stress and strain of modern life does not help one to achieve it. We must train our actor to achieve it on the stage otherwise he will be stiff and wooden or clumsy and awkward of gait.

Stage movement has to be adjusted to the actual space available. In a multi-roomed tenement setting such as that of *The Diary of Anne Frank* he will find that his movements are restricted by a small acting area and a good deal of furniture. On the other hand in *Othello* or *Hamlet* he may find himself lost on a stage which appears huge to him. In each case he must adjust his movements to the acting space at his disposal.

To obtain control over the body requires subjection to a routine of exercises and activities. These help one to achieve freedom from tension and to acquire a sense of rhythm. Dancing, fencing, eurythmics and games all help in this respect.

Does physical stature play a large part in determining the success of the actor? Very little on the whole. There have been many great artists of small build. Others have been fat, thin and even deformed. When asked this question one can think of Raimu and Charlie Chaplin, both great artists in spite of their physical limitations or even because of them. Heroic parts, juvenile leads and certain character roles may demand certain physical attributes, but these are not always the most interesting roles in the theatre.

It is a truism that the inexperienced performer does not know what to do with his hands. Sometimes he will take the easy way and put them in his pockets. On other occasions he will pluck up courage and point or saw the air to underline every sentence. The co-ordination of gesture and speech is another problem which he must solve. Again it is a question of control of the body and the acquisition of a general sense of rhythm.

In this country in normal conversation the use of gesture is reduced to a minimum. Other nations make it an expressive accompaniment to every-day speech. In France or Italy it is not considered incongruous to keep the hands and arms in perpetual motion while speaking whereas here it would be thought ludicrous. In former times the British socialite was not exempt from similar habits. Bowing with figure of eight gestures, the lady's use of the fan—these were the regular by-play of conversation of the haut-monde of a by-gone age. All these modes and manners may have to be brought to life again on the stage and not appear unnatural or out of place with their surroundings. This requires constant practice and long rehearsals.

INNER TECHNIQUE

However much the actor may have tuned up and trained his body to meet the demands made upon it by the stage task, it will be but an empty shell if it is not supported by an Inner Technique of comparable excellence. The voice, movement and gesture are means of communication. They are useless unless there is something to communicate. That something is the author's script re-inforced by the thoughts and feelings of the interpreter.

Imagination is a necessary part of the equipment. It helps him to transform himself into a Hamlet, a Lear or a more mundane surburban householder. Imagination tells him that all the events of the play could happen to him because they are within the realm of human experience. His performance is thereby enriched.

There is another quality, akin to imagination, which is of great help in the preparation of a role. This is creative fantasy.

Creative fantasy helps to give the semblance of life to events or things which could not possibly have happened to you. The witches in *Macbeth*, Caesar's ghost and many of the murders which permeate the Drama, are outside the reach of the ordinary person's experience. To believe in them the actor must assume the naiveté of the child who believes in fairies. He must say, "If this happened to me I should . . ." The answer will be in accordance with the role he has assumed. "If" is a magic word, as Stanlislavsky was quick to point out. With it the most prosaic surroundings are transformed to the cloud capped towers of

Ilium, to gorgeous palaces and to the immensity of the great globe itself.

Concentration is as necessary to the actor as it is to the mathematician. Too much awareness of the audience destroys concentration and fosters a diffused type of attention, which in turn leads to the muzzy performace. A performer who looks through his stage partner instead of looking at him, the performer who does not listen to what his partner is saying—both are guilty of lacking the type of concentration we require.

Is intelligence part of the equipment? Yes, but it is a special type of intuitive intelligence—one that opens for him the door to the secrets of emotional conflict, of human motives. Reason, logic, precise cause and effect play little part in it. Very often he reaches the heart of the matter of an emotional sequence without knowing the reason; and perhaps this is as it should be. His job is to act.

SUMMARY

The general requirements of the actor are summarised in this diagram.

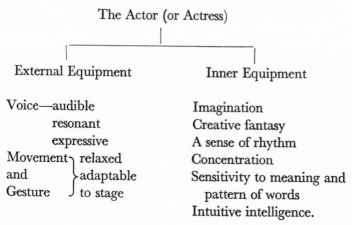

The Actor (or Actress)

External Equipment	Inner Equipment
Voice—audible	Imagination
resonant	Creative fantasy
expressive	A sense of rhythm
Movement┐ relaxed	Concentration
and ├ adaptable	Sensitivity to meaning and
Gesture ┘ to stage	pattern of words
	Intuitive intelligence.

★ 3 ★

Establishing Contact with the Audience

WHAT should be the correct attitude of the actor towards his audience? Stanislavsky held that the spectator should be a privileged observer. This is hardly feasible when the actor is the Prologue or Narrator and makes the initial impact on the audience. His task is threefold: to introduce the audience to the story; to put the listener in the right mood to listen and appreciate it; and lastly, to accept the challenge that every audience offers to him. For challenge it is. The first impression often makes the play—if it misfires the whole performance may suffer.

The object of these preliminary experiments is to help the student performer to obtain an easy and friendly attitude towards his audience. This can be a very difficult task; the beginner is often awkward and self-conscious to such a degree that the flow of performance from artist to audience is greatly impeded. Tensions, facial contortions and jerky movements are the result and are easier to cure once the cause—a deep seated fear of the audience—has been removed. General exercises in relaxation are of great help but cannot in most cases be considered the complete answer to the problem. The two experiments here described should prove useful to supplement any good "loosening-up" or relaxation routine.

EXPERIMENT 1.   AIM: TO TELL THE STORY

Number involved: One performer and a class of 12 acting as an audience. Each member of the class is in turn the performer.

The Narrator: "My father's family name being Pirrip, and my Christian name Phillip, my infant tongue could make of both names nothing longer or more explicit than Pip. So I called myself Pip, and came to be called Pip.

I gave Pirrip as my father's family name on the authority of his tombstone and my sister—Mrs. Joe Gargery—who was more than twenty years older than me and married to the blacksmith. As I never saw my father or my mother and never saw any likeness of either of them—for their days were long before the days of photographs—my first fancies regarding what they were like were unreasonably derived from their tombstone. The shape of the letters on my father's gave me an odd idea that he was a square, stout, dark man with curly black hair. From the character and turn of the inscription 'Also Georgiana, Wife of the Above' I drew a childlike conclusion that my mother was freckled and sickly.

Ours was the marsh country, down by the river, within, as the river wound, twenty miles of the sea. My first most vivid impression of the identity of things seems to me to have been gained on a memorable raw afternoon towards evening. At such a time I found out for certain that this bleak place, overgrown with nettles, was the church yard, and that the dark, flat wilderness beyond that church yard, intersected with dykes and mounds and gates, with scattered cattle feeding on it, was the marshes, and that the low leaden line beyond was the river; and that the distant savage lair from which the wind was rushing was the sea. With the cold realisation of this I began to cry."

Great Expectations—by Charles Dickens.

Directions given to the Performer.

Read this passage silently to yourself and study it. Imagine that you are the Narrator or Prologue and that it is your task to introduce the audience to the background to this story in a simple and straightforward manner. Try to imagine that you are

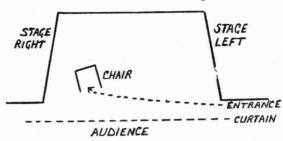

Fig. 1

reading it under actual conditions of the theatre. On stage there is a chair which is set close to the footlights on stage right. You are in the wings ready to take your place while the Orchestra is finishing the overture. A short piece of introductory music is played as the curtain rises on a dimly lit stage. Enter from stage left carrying your book, and walk towards the chair. When you reach it pause and wait for a spotlight to come up on you. Then slowly, without fuss, lift the book and look at its cover to ascertain that you have brought the right one, sit down, turn to the required page, look up at the audience, smile (using your eyes), lift the book and quietly begin to tell us the story. Don't worry about making the wrong move. The instructor will prompt you on what to do next if you forget.

Here is the sequence once more:

1. The Overture ends.
2. The houselights fade and the introductory music is played.
3. The curtain rises.
4. You enter and walk towards the chair.
5. Stop at the chair.
6. Wait for the spot to come up on you.
7. Look at the book.
8. Sit down.
9. Turn to the required page (which is marked).
10. Acknowledge the audience with your eyes.

11. Lift the book.
12. Tell us the story.

The Performance.

The performer then reads the passage, without interruptions from the instructor or 'audience'.

Further Directions.

If the performer is nervous or hesitant he is asked to repeat the performance with the minimum of criticism of the first attempt. Common errors are pointed out to the performer before the second attempt is made. Detailed criticism is not given at this stage so as not to impair the student's confidence.

Comments.

The various actions to be done before the reading actually begins helps the performer to feel at home on the stage and then to establish direct contact with the audience without posing or over-acting. Whispered directions to less confident students do not usually break the continuity of the performance.

Common Errors.

1. Speaking too fast—this is usually due to nervousness and is normally rectified in the second attempt.
2. Over-dramatising. The passage chosen requires straight narrative treatment. This fault again was normally put right in the next performance.
3. Bad sight-reading—Students should be given five minutes to study the passage in order to prevent the experiment lapsing into a sight reading exercise. Bad reading is caused by diffused attention which causes hesitation and stumbling. The most successful method of cure I have attempted is to hold my hand above my head about 15 feet in front of the performer, and to

ask him to read towards it. In many cases this helps the student to focus his attention in one direction and thereby give a firmer quality to the reading.

Supplementary Exercises.

The following passages are to be treated in the same way. If possible variations to the above routine should be introduced so as to prevent it becoming a rubber stamp method for the student who will eventually evolve his own personal routine for establishing contact with his audience.

Exercise 1.

This might be an introduction to a play about the second world war.

Narrator: This is a story about ordinary people—men and women you meet every day. You may see some of them in your home town, going about their everyday business without calling attention to themselves. One of them might be the neighbour you speak to over the garden fence. Another the friendly person you have invited home for a cup of tea. None of them is anybody special. It might be you or I.

The story began some time ago, when Europe was at war, and honour and decency were fighting for survival against the forces of evil and brutality.

It is your story, listen to it . . .

Exercise 2.

The Prologue to the medieval morality play 'Everyman'.
I pray you all give your audience,
And hear this matter with reverence,
In figure a moral play.
'The Summoning of Everyman' called it is,
That of our lives and ending shews
How transitory we be all day.
This matter is wondrous precious;
But the intent of it is more gracious
And sweet to bear away.

The story saith:—Man, in the beginning
Look well, and take good heed to the ending
Be you never so gay!
Ye think sin in the beginning full sweet,
Which in the end causeth the soul to weep
When the body lyeth in clay.
Here shall you see how Fellowship and Jollity,
Both Strength, Pleasure and Beauty,
Will fade from thee as flowers in May;
For ye shall hear how our heavenly king
Calleth Everyman to a general reckoning.
Give audience, and hear what he doth say.

(Author anonymous).

Here the verse is not difficult to speak and the language has a simplicity and directness which makes it very suitable for getting straight to the heart of the listener.

Exercise 3.

The Chorus from "Romeo and Juliet".
Two households, both alike in dignity,
In fair Verona, where we lay our scene,
From ancient grudge break to new mutiny,
Where civil blood makes civil hands unclean.
From forth the fatal loins of these two foes
A pair of star-cross'd lovers take their life;
Whose misadventur'd piteous overthrows
Do with their death bury their parents' strife.
The fearful passage of their death-mark'd love,
And the continuance of their parents' rage,
Which, but their children's end, nought could remove,
Is now the two hours' traffick of our stage;
The which, if you with patient ears attend,
What here shall miss, our toil shall strive to mend."

(*William Shakespeare*).

This is a masterly summary of the story of the play and every line must *tell*. The problem is one of not over-dramatising a fundamentally dramatic tale.

EXPERIMENT 2. AIM: TO EXCITE THE AUDIENCE

Number involved: 1 performer:—12 in audience.

Material used: The Prologue to Henry V.

In these examples instead of the gentle approach to the audience a more forceful attitude is required. The extract is learnt beforehand.

> O! for a Muse of fire, that would ascend
> The brightest heaven of invention;
> A kingdom for a stage, princes to act
> And monarchs to behold the swelling scene.
> Then should the warlike Harry, like himself,
> Assume the port of Mars: and at his heels,
> Leash'd in like hounds, should famine, sword, and fire
> Crouch for employment. But pardon, gentles all,
> The flat unraised spirits that hath dar'd
> On this unworthy scaffold to bring forth
> So great an object: can this cockpit hold
> The vasty fields of France? or may we cram
> Within this wooden O the very casques
> That did affright the air at Agincourt?
> O, pardon! since a crooked figure may
> Attest in little place a million;
> And let us, ciphers to this great accompt,
> On your imaginary forces work.
>
> (*William Shakespeare*).

Furniture Required.

On stage: Nil.

In auditorium: Three chairs, placed at the back of the hall, one each on the left and right, and one in the centre.

Directions given.

Imagine that the curtain is rising to a martial roll of drums, on a fully lit stage. You enter from Up Stage Centre and advance with confident steps towards the audience. Halt Down Stage Centre and adopt a firm stance (legs astride, hands on hips).

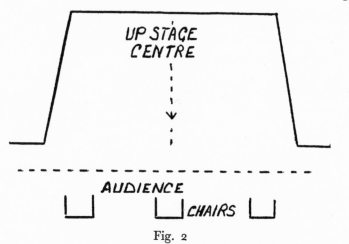

Fig. 2

Look at the centre chair and confidently and clearly address your remarks to it. As the speech progresses, when the text calls for a change, address one of the other chairs. Do this again when another change is required. Remember it is your job to arouse the audience's interest and enthusiasm. Move from one part of the stage to another if it helps you to 'win over' other members of the audience.

Notes:

1. If the performer makes a false start, which usually means his employing insufficient attack, he is asked to start again. A third attempt will be required in one or two cases.
2. The chairs are occupied by members of the audience only when it is certain that the placing of people well known to them in these key positions does not 'put off' the performers.

Comments.

The deploying of the actor's focus of attention by means of the three chairs helps him to vary the performance. As a producer I have often been struck by some artist's reluctance to face towards the audience when the action requires it. This exercise can cure the inhibitive tendency to avoid the audience; the performer must play out because he has something or someone to play to. The resultant danger of the artist always playing out towards the audience in comic opera fashion does not arise if the subsequent training stresses playing to the stage partner. Incidentally the dictum that you must always face the person to whom you are speaking is a fallacious one; there are occasions when turning the head away is dramatically more effective.

N.B. The special problems relating to the speaking of Dramatic Verse and to Shakespearian acting should not be dealt with at this stage as they might obscure the main purpose of the exercise which is to excite the audience.

Common Errors.

1. Forcing the voice. This points to the fact that this exercise should be attempted when an advanced stage has been reached in the Vocal Training. Breath control exercises and singing of the first words of the passage around the middle of the students' range help to eliminate this fault. (see page 143).

2. Jerky movements. Requiring long-term treatment in the movement class. Relaxation exercises and a movement routine such as the one described on pages 119-123 will help to ensure smooth and clean-cut movements.

Supplementary Exercises.

The following speeches require a similarly robust treatment:

Exercise 4.

The Speaker: Here you, listen! Stop snoring in your seats or rattling your teacups. Yes, listen! Men are dying while you sleep—women are thirsting while you drink . . . You, and you and you, wake up!

This can be used for the more timid student who cannot yet sustain a longer speech. It aims to rouse the audience to a state of receptivity.

Exercise 5. The Induction to Henry IV, Part II.

Rumour: Open your ears; for which of you will stop
The vent of hearing when loud Rumour speaks?
I, from the orient to the drooping west,
Making the wind my post-horse, still unfold
The acts commenced on this ball of earth:
Upon my tongues continual slanders ride,
The which in every language I pronounce,
Stuffing the ears of men with false reports.

(William Shakespeare).

The urgency of the reports which Rumour is disseminating call for a quick tempo delivery of these lines. This is difficult for the beginner who tends to gabble, thereby losing the gist of the speech. A good piece of advice is—start by saying the lines slowly and when you feel confident begin to let the urgency of the speech make you gather momentum. Do not sacrifice meaning to pace.

Exercise 6.

The Speaker: This is war. Beat the drum. Blow the trumpet. Let the whole world know that I, Sam Knowles, am going into battle. Blow your trumpets, Angels, around earth's imagined corners. Let the forces of evil tremble; they are my first target. Right men, ready?—take aim—Fire.

The scene begins with a tour de force—guns aimed at the audience, as it were. The student must let himself go without losing control of his voice, movements or gestures. The passage should be employed—

1.   As an exercise for contacting the audience by giving it an initial shock.

2. As an exercise in control by varying the movements to take in the three observers in the chairs.

3. As a vocal exercise when the student has learnt to increase the volume of his voice without strain or shouting.

SUMMARY

Direct contact with the audience must be achieved by the prologue or narrator of the play. The threefold task of the prologue is—

1. to introduce the audience to the story,
2. to put the listener in the right frame of mind,
3. to accept the challenge of being the first one of the cast to face the audience.

The object of the experiments is to make the beginner less self conscious and to help him be at home with his audience. Together with the exercises they should supplement movement and loosening up routines.

Two types of exercises are described; the first requiring a gentle approach and the second a forceful, more robust attitude.

Acting with a Partner

Every producer, every teacher of drama, is faced at some time
or other with the problem of the student who cannot act with a
stage partner and whose performance is akin to a series of operatic
arias, without relevance to the other person's contribution.
When two such people are on the stage together the effect obtained is similar to that of certain passages in *Comic Opera*
where the audience is regaled with the thoughts of two performers who seem to be insistent upon putting forward their own
point of view at the expense of that of their partner. A stage
duologue is comparable to a game of tennis—one must give as
well as take. The actor who has learned to listen without strain,
to act to his partner's eyes, has solved this problem of establishing
contact with the other members of the team. This quality is
usually called "giving": it is often lacking in beginners for a
variety of reasons. In weekly repertory theatres where the lines
have been incompletely learnt, the hesitant mind of the artist
groping for the author's words, prevents him from establishing
contact both with his partner and with his audience. Muscular
tension is another common cause of this fault. On the other hand,
the ability to relax and become absorbed in the play encourages
"giving".

Shakespeare provides abundant material to illustrate the
necessity for giving and taking. This passage from *Macbeth* is an
excellent example:

Macbeth	My dearest love,

Duncan comes here tonight.

Lady Macbeth And when goes hence?

Macbeth   To-morrow, as he purposes.

Lady Macbeth   Oh never

Shall sun that morrow see.
Your face, my thane, is as a book where men
May read strange matters.

Taken in the light of the fact that Macbeth must have already considered the murder of Duncan and that Lady Macbeth has decided to spur him on to the deed, it is easy to realise that she has here read his unspoken thoughts. The actress who speaks the last three lines without receiving these unuttered thoughts from her partner will have failed to interpret the author's intention. So will the actor who plays Macbeth if he does not transmit to his partner what is in his mind when he says, "To-morrow, as he purposes."

Words can often be a hindrance to complete communication. As we shall see later when dealing with charged dialogue, they often belie their surface meaning. This experiment dispenses with dialogue in order to free the beginner from the additional problems which speech poses:

EXPERIMENT 3. AIM: TO ESTABLISH CONTACT WITH THE STAGE PARTNER

Number involved: 2 performers (1m. 1f.)
Furniture required:

    1 cabinet U.R.
    1 table L.C.
    1 chair D.L. of table
    Mantelpiece L.
    Door U.R.

The Characters: The husband. The wife.

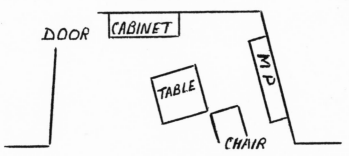

Fig. 3
Layout of Furniture.

Directions to "A" (The husband)

You have quarrelled with your wife this morning and she
has retired to this room where she is sitting on the chair D.L.
reading a book. You now want to "make-up" and you regret
all those harsh words you have spoken. Enter the room by door
U.R., pour out a drink for yourself and another for her without
speaking; try to attract her attention and establish good relations
with her. The properties (imaginary) on stage—bottles and
glasses in the cabinet U.R. You can if you wish, as a last resort,
make use of pencil and paper. As each attempt fails try and
think of something else, if necessary walking about while you are
doing so . . .

Directions to "B" (The wife)

Do all you can to resist his overtures until the instructor gives
you the signal to "give in", so that the scene ends in your being
reconciled to each other.

Notes:

1. After the first performance the roles are exchanged, and it is
the wife's turn to attempt to conciliate the husband.
2. For younger students (e.g. 11 or 12 years) the persons involved

4

are two school friends who have quarrelled. Different properties (toys, sweets, etc.) are used in this case.

Comments.

This exercise has been tried with students of varying ages and on practically every occasion it was successful, insofar as the students were

1. absorbed in the stage tasks.

2. by the very nature of the plot were obliged to try and establish or resist contact with each other. Thus even the passive performer was really playing together with the stage partner.

The following are descriptions of two examples of imaginative performances:

1. The repentant husband who brought his wife a cushion which he placed behind her back and then stood looking over her shoulder until she turned away. He then paused, crossed to the mantlepiece, lit two cigarettes, came back to her and placed one in her mouth. Even this touching demonstration of marital devotion was accepted with indifference by his obdurate spouse. It was only when he went to the door and paused to give one last dejected look at his wife, with the expression of a guilty schoolboy, that her resistance was broken; she suddenly smiled and then ran to him amid the applause of those watching. In this case my signal for the reconciliation was not required.

2. The schoolboy of twelve who regained his fellow's friendship by offering him his favourite toy, a model aeroplane. His miming was excellent and the other boy sat transfixed as he watched the imaginary plane fly round the room. When he realised that this was to be his own property, his amazement and joy broke down all resistance to the re-establishment of their friendship.

Common Errors.

1. Hurrying through the performance. When this happened I instructed that each unsuccessful attempt be punctuated by a pause during which the conciliator asked himself the question, "What am I to do next?" He was then obliged to find an answer in his mind before translating it into action. This had the effect of slowing down the performance and making it more convincing.
2. The 'resistor' anticipating the other person's advances before the overture was made. When pointed out this fault was soon corrected.

Supplementary exercises.

Exercise 1. A Scene of Parting.

"A" (man) and "B" (woman) are meeting for the last time. She looks at his face and sees in it his resolution not to see her again.

B. So this is goodbye.

A. I'm afraid it is.

She attempts to reach out to him. He turns away. Her hand drops. There is a pause as she looks at his back, stiff with determination. Then, in an effort to control her tears she runs off.

Here the attempt to establish sympathetic contact must be made by the woman. The man resists and only when the finality of her failure is brought home does she make her exit.

The performers change places and it is the woman's turn to be the resolute one.

Exercise 2.

"A" and "B" face each other. Without using speech "A" will attempt to communicate the following to "B".

I love you.

I hate you.

Why did you do it?
I pity you.
I sympathise with you.
I don't know what to say.
There's something wrong.

"B" will then try to guess what "A" has been trying to communicate. The usual fault here is for the students to stare at each other and to try too hard. The result is excessive muscular constriction and grimacing. The actor must prepare himself by thinking what he is trying to say; this can be easily done by relating it to a particular situation, e.g. the circumstances which result in "A" saying "I hate you", might be harm done to his family, a false accusation, or a betrayal of trust.

Exercise 3.

X is visiting Y in prison. The presence of the warder acts as a restraining influence. Determine the circumstances which have led to his conviction. It may be for theft or because he is shielding someone else. Improvise the dialogue. Remember that you have not seen each other for a long time. This requires giving and taking during the silent moments and during speech. A similar situation occurs in Act IV of Arthur Miller's *The Crucible* when John Proctor is visited by his wife in prison after they have been parted for several months.

Exercise 4.

From the *Alcestis* of Euripides—translated by Gilbert Murray.
Alcestis has sacrificed herself for her husband Admetus by taking his place when his time has come to die. However she is rescued by Heracles, who is here about to reveal to Admetus that the strange veiled woman is really his wife:
Heracles brings the woman close to Admetus, who looks determinedly away. She reaches out her arms.

Admetus I touch her not. Let her go in.

Heracles   I am loth
    To trust her save to thy pledged hand and oath.
    (He lays his hand on Admetus's shoulder)

Admetus (desperately) Lord, this is violence . . . wrong . . .

Heracles   Reach forth thine hand
    and touch this comer from a distant land.

Admetus (holding out his hand without looking)
    Like Perseus when he touched the Gorgon, there!

Heracles Thou hast touched her?

Admetus (at last touching her hand) Touched her? . . . Yes.

Heracles (a hand on the shoulder of each)
                                    Then cling to her;
    And say if thou hast found a guest of grace
    In God's son Heracles! (He removes her veil)
                                  Look in her face;
    Look; is she like . . . ?
    (Admetus looks and stands amazed).
                              Go and forget in bliss
    Thy sorrow!

Admetus   Oh ye Gods! What meaneth this?
    A marvel beyond dreams! The face . . . 'tis she;
    Mine, verily mine! Or doth God mock at me
    And blast my vision with some mad surmise?

Heracles Not so. This is thy wife before thine eyes.

    Here the actor playing Heracles has the task of communicating
to Admetus what the latter half suspects, i.e. that the strange lady
is his wife. The moment of revelation when the veil is removed is
the climax of the scene and is marked by the speechlessness of
Admetus at the miracle which has occurred. Alcestis herself
should radiate affection for Admetus and this is also shown by
her stretching out her arms towards him.

SUMMARY

1. When acting with a stage partner it is necessary to 'give' and 'take'.

2. By *giving* is meant transmitting one's own thoughts and feelings to the partner. This helps to establish *contact* with him and prevents the mechanical repetition of the lines of the text.

3. It is necessary to discover what lies behind the words of text and to communicate this to the partner and to the audience.

4. It is helpful to act to the partner's eyes, even when one is not looking at him.

5. By *taking* is meant listening to the partner and receiving the latter's thoughts and feelings.

6. The scene between Macbeth and his wife in which unspoken thoughts have to be transmitted and received can serve as a valuable exercise in giving and taking.

7. Isolated or selfish acting impedes contact with the other people on the stage.

8. Experiment 3 (a reconciliation scene) and the supplementary exercises aim to help the actor to avoid isolated acting.

★ 5 ★

Sense and Emotion

The Use of the Senses.

WE have already noted that Imagination is an essential part of the actor's equipment. How is he to develop it to enrich his work? One fertile source is practice in the use of his five senses: sight, hearing, touch, taste and smell. Personal experiences in which any of these senses have been employed will help him when he is studying his role. The most important senses for this purpose are those of sight and hearing. Individuals vary in the use of them in everyday life. Some people re-act more sharply to the things they see and others to the sounds they hear. Psychologists divide them into types endowed with visual or auditive imagery.

Stanislavsky in *An Actor Prepares* says "Actors have this same kind of power (*as that of other artists*) of recalling images of sight and sound. Actors of the visual memory type like to see what is wanted of them and then their emotions respond easily. Others much prefer to hear the sound of the voice or the intonation of the person they are to portray. With them their first impulse to feeling comes from their auditive memories."

The other senses, although often considered less important than sight and hearing, have their part to play in the creation of certain roles. When portraying a blind man the sense of touch is important, as in *The Paragon* by Roland and Michael Pertwee, where the blind father plays a major role in the development and the tragic ending of the drama. The sense of smell plays a vital part in the gas filled apartment of Hester Collyer in the first act of *The Deep Blue Sea*, and who could play the part of Falstaff without that sense of taste which relishes the oft called for pot of sack.

Emotion Memory.

Emotion Memory is the term we use for the recall of emotions we have experienced in the past. The attendant details of an accident—blood or a battered car or an injured man—may make an emotional impact on us which is easily recalled when similar details are described in a play. After a time these details filter through the mind of the artist who selects those he can reproduce in performance. All artists, poets, painters or musicians utilise this process. Wordsworth speaks of "emotion recollected in tranquillity". He, too, pre-supposes time as the filter of our emotional experiences.

Dramatists give their characters ample opportunity to speak of the past. Ibsen's Master Builder tells Hilde of the tragic chain of events which led to the loss of his children: in *Rebecca* by Daphne du Maurier there is a similar description by Max de Winter of the circumstances which led to his murdering his first wife; in the *Deep Blue Sea* Hester Collyer tells her husband how she fell in love with Freddie—as she does so she re-lives the past. Othello's speech to the Senate is another example. There are many others.

In Experiment 4. I tried to help the actor to use his Emotion Memory when acting a simple scene. I have used it with students ranging from 12 year olds to adults. It should test the actor's imaginative ability to re-create the past and should help him to transmit his experience to the audience.

EXPERIMENT 4. AIM: TO GIVE PRACTICE IN THE USE OF EMOTION MEMORY

Number involved: 1 performer.

Furniture required:

1 table.

1 desk.

1 rocking chair—or substitute.

1 chair.

1 chest.

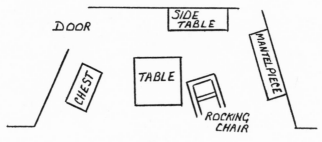

Fig. 4

Plan of furniture:

Directions given beforehand.

You are to enter a room where you spent many happy (or unhappy) years some time ago. In it are several objects (imaginary) to remind you of those years. Thus on the mantelpiece (L.) there is an old smelly pipe and near it a photograph. There is a rickety table in the centre of the room and to the left of it an old rocking chair. On a side table (U.L.) can be seen a seashell and a book (perhaps a Bible) which somebody you knew then used to read. There is a chest (R.C.) filled with the very clothes you wore for charades. Notice these things one by one, touch them and handle them as you remember their place in your past. It does not matter if you do not remember all these objects. In your imagination place as many of them as possible in parts of the room as they occur to you. Make up some of your own, if necessary.

Directions given during the experiment consisted of whispered suggestions as to the next move when the student appeared to be hesitant. They were delivered in the general evocative mood of the scene.

Comments.

This experiment was a great success with students of all ages. I find it to be one of the easiest methods of achieving complete absorption in the stage task. Over-acting very rarely occurs and only slight adjustments related to external technique are sometimes required to transmit the performers' reactions to the audience.

It is interesting to compare some of the performances. I describe four of them by my former students as examples of imaginative work.

1. A boy of 12 showed surprise which changed to delight at finding his favourite toy, a miniature car, which he wound up and pushed along the floor.

2. A girl of 13 hated the room. A photograph reminded her of someone whom she obviously disliked. Each object was seen and handled as though it brought back an unhappy incident in the child's life.

3. A girl of 17 entered the room rather waif-like and paused in wonder. She hardly dared to touch the objects. To her the happy past was too painful to recall because of the unhappy present. This was a most moving performance.

4. A woman of forty steeled herself to look. She touched the pipe as though it were a treasured object and collapsed on the chair in despair—she then allowed its rocking movement to soothe her. In this case the technical ability of the actress ensured good timing and the performance was much enriched.

Common Errors.

1. Hiding the facial reaction from the audience by continually facing upstage. I did not correct this fault in cases where I felt that over-awareness of technical niceties would impede absorption in the scene. When a more advanced stage has been reached, the instructor should demonstrate how to turn towards the audience as an object "registers". This strengthens the impact on the observer.

2. Too frequent head turns. This is another common error with beginners whose jerky head movements detract from the sincerity of the performance. This fault can be remedied by slowing down the general pace and lengthening the gaps between recognition of individual objects.

3. Hurrying through the stage task. This is due to nervousness coupled with the desire to get it over quickly. Here again directions to slow down the pace tempered with judicious advice from the instructor during the performance usually has the required effect of adding conviction.

Supplementary Exercises.

A. *The Use of the Five Senses.*

1. *Sight.* Scan the horizon for the plane, now long overdue, which is carrying somebody you know (a husband, wife, mother, father).

Look for the purse which you have left somewhere in the room.

Examine the handwriting of a document which you think is forged.

2. *Hearing.* Try to distinguish between the footsteps of different people you know.

Improvise a telephone conversation with an imaginary person and try to hear his replies.

Listen for the sound of (a) a scream (b) the cry of a child, (c) the door bell, (d) a motor horn, (e) a dog barking. Try to fit these sounds into scenes made up by yourself.

3. *Touch*. Imagine that you are blind. Walk around the room as though you knew where everything was situated. Sit down in your favourite chair, smoke a cigarette or pipe.

4. *Taste*. Drink an imaginary cup of tea, a glass of beer or a glass of water.

Imagine that you are very hungry—mime the eating of the meal when it is finally served.

5. *Smell*. Imagine that you can smell (a) something burning, (b) coal gas, (c) a savoury dish, (d) a cheap perfume. (e) the sea.

The authenticity of the performance when these exercises are practised should be checked by the instructor. Overacting should immediately be pointed out.

Emotion Memory.

Exercise 1.

Describe in your own words any incident which has made a profound impression on you. The rest of the class is to act as an audience.

In this exercise do not worry about the fluency of your speech and do not be afraid of pausing if necessary.

Exercise 2.

From *Look Back in Anger* by John Osborne, Act II, Sc. I. Alison is telling her friend Helena how she first met Jimmy Porter.

Alison. I met him at a party. I remember it so clearly. I was almost twenty-one. The men there all looked as though they distrusted him, and as for the women, they were all intent on showing their contempt for this rather odd creature but no one seemed quite sure how to do it. He'd come to the party on a bicycle, he told me, and there was oil over his dinner jacket. It had been such a lovely day, and he'd been in the sun. Everything about him seemed to burn, his face, the edges of his hair glistened and seemed to

spring off his head, and his eyes were so blue and full of
the sun. He looked so young and frail, in spite of the tired
line of his mouth. I knew that I was taking on more than
I was ever likely to be capable of bearing, but there never
seemed to be any choice . . .

Compare this was Hester Collyer's speech in Act II of *The
Deep Blue Sea*, in which she tells of her first meeting with Freddie.
It begins, "And Freddie and I sat on the veranda together for
at least an hour" . . . and ends, ". . . I knew then in that tiny
moment when we were laughing together so close that I had
no hope. No hope at all."

Exercise 3. From *Anthony and Cleopatra.*

(Enobarbus's description of his first sight of Cleopatra.)

Enobarbus.   The barge she sat in, like a burnished throne,
                Burnt on the water: the poop was beaten gold,
                Purple the sails: and so perfumed that
                The winds were love-sick.
                With them the oars were silver,
                Which to the tune of flutes kept stroke, and made
                The water which they beat, to follow faster;
                As amorous of their strokes. For her own person,
                It beggar'd all description, she did lie
                In her pavilion, cloth of gold, of tissue,
                O'er picturing that Venus, where we see
                The fancy out-work nature.

To say the least, that first impression of Cleopatra must have
lingered in his memory.

Exercise 4. From *Uncle Vanya* by Anton Chekhov. Act II.

Voynitsky (Uncle Vanya) in this soliloquy, explains why life
has passed him by.

Voynitsky: Oh, how I've been cheated! I worshipped the Professor, that gout-ridden old crock, and slaved like an ox for him. Sonya and I squeezed the last drop out of the estate. Like grasping Kulaks we traded in linseed oil, peas and curds. We went short of food to scrape our farthings together and send him thousands of roubles. I was proud of him and his learning. I lived and breathed only for him. Everything he wrote or uttered seemed to me to have the touch of genius . . . My God, and now? Now he's retired. Now one can see the sum total of his life. When he goes not one page of his writing will survive. He's completely unknown—a nobody, a soap bubble. And I've been cheated—I see it now—stupidly cheated.

This speech inspired by self-pitying despair proves to be a valuable exercise in emotion memory.

Other Passages from modern plays are:

Laura. Loving you is hard for me . . . and I don't know what to do.   (*Still Life*—Noel Coward)

Max. I hated her . . . When I killed her she was smiling still.   (*Rebecca*—Act III Daphne du Maurier).

Bessie. Ralphie, I worked too hard all my life to be treated like dirt . . . Talk from now to next year—this is life in America.   (*Awake and Sing*—Clifford Odets)

SUMMARY

1. The five senses (sight, hearing, touch, taste and smell) help the actor to enrich his imagination.

2. Sight and hearing are the most important. Some actors have a stronger visual memory while others have a stronger auditive memory.

3. The other senses often have an important part to play (e.g. the sense of smell in Act I of *The Deep Blue Sea*).

4. By *emotion memory* is meant the recall of feelings and emotions experienced in the past. Our senses help us to do this sincerely. The actor selects certain details from his store of emotional experiences and reproduces these details in performance.

5. Many plays contain passages which recall past emotions experienced by the characters. Several examples are given here. They provide useful practical exercises in the use of emotion memory.

⋆ 6 ⋆

Quarrel Scenes

THE stage quarrel if inexpertly handled can be a source of embarrassment to both actor and audience. I still have painful memories of a rehearsal in weekly repertory when the producer gave me instructions to "top" (speak louder than) the other performer during a stage quarrel which lasted several minutes, the idea being that the louder we shouted, the more effective would be the scene. The result was a strained voice, two unhappy performers and as I learned later, an unhappy audience.

Major and Minor Climaxes.

Scenes of sharp conflict should be studied and rehearsed so as to bring out the minor climaxes which are normally present. The producer and actor should detect these in the script and use them to lead up to the main climax of the sustained quarrel. They must remember that after tension comes relaxation, because both actor and audience need a breather before the next sequence of dramatic tension builds up. Here again the master dramatist helps his performer. The Cassius-Brutus tent scene from *Julius Caesar* (Act IV., Sc. III) is a shining example of the building up to a major climax through several subsidiary curves of action, followed by a subsiding to a gentler mood. Again, the second act of Noel Coward's *Private Lives* is almost in its entirety a sustained quarrel and this too repays study as a series of exchanges leading up to climaxes. Perhaps one of the best quarrel scenes of recent

years was in Clifford Odets' *Winter Journey* when the insults hurled
at the harassed wife of dipsomaniac actor by a distraught stage
producer end in the inevitable result—his face was slapped.

Attitude to the Partner.

In quarrel scenes it is even more important to establish contact
with one's partner than in other duologues. The actor must learn
to possess sufficient control, even at the height of the quarrel, to
attempt to communicate to his fellow what he himself is thinking
or, more often, feeling. Uncontrolled shouting is a hindrance to
this and should be ruled out. In the initial stages of rehearsal
these scenes will often be untidy and over-played. It is then the
producer's task to orchestrate the complete performance and
assign to each participant his due share in the scene as a whole.
When more than two people are taking part the producer's task
is more difficult and doubly important.

When helping a performer in these scenes he should be asked
to give himself a definite reason for speaking as he does to his
antagonist. This he can do by saying to himself, "I want to make
him realise . . ." or "I want to punish him for . . ." Similar
beginnings to complete sentences, if continued according to the
situation in the play, can help him to determine the correct
meaning, pace and emphasis of the spoken words and, what is
more fundamental, to determine the correct attitude to the person
he is addressing.

Experiment 5 was undertaken in order to find a method of
accustoming students to the general rhythm of a quarrel sequence
involving two persons. It was not meant to be a rubber-stamp
method for the treatment of all such sequences. I found it
successful in combating the inartistic, "louder-still-and-louder"
type of treatment.

EXPERIMENT 5. *A Quarrel Sequence.*

AIM: TO DISCOVER AN APPROACH TO THE ACTING OF QUARREL SCENES

Number involved: Two students.

The situation: An accusation of theft.

Furniture required: 1 table. 1 armchair.

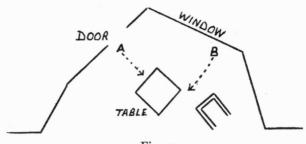

Fig. 5

Plan of furniture:

Directions given.

B. is discovered on stage U.L. by the window. A. enters by door R. He is obviously angry and his first words are, "You haven't told me the truth". B. turns and says "How dare you". A. approaches table from R. continuing the quarrel, improvising the words.

B. then approaches the table from L. They continue the quarrel facing each other across the table. The climax is reached when A. slaps table with his hand shouting, "You're a thief". There is a pause as they look at each other. B. then slowly turns away, walks to the armchair and collapses into it.

Notes:

1. If there is difficulty in improvising the words aloud it will be found that the continuation of the quarrel in a whisper does not

usually interrupt the flow of the performance. However the key sentences mentioned above should be spoken aloud.

2. The situation can be varied with different key sentences which should be fairly short so that very little memorising is required.

Variations in movement should be attempted, remembering that for the purpose of this exercise the general sequence is:

i. Initial sentence.
ii. Reaction (by B.).
iii. Approaching move by A.
iv. Approaching move by B.
v. No movement with an obstacle (the table) between them and yet building up to the climax.
vi. The climax—the bang on the table, a blow or a word.
vii. Pause—the tension point.
viii. Release of tension by a gesture or move in a more restrained mood.

Comments.

Despite the fact that only the framework was given, the essence of the quarrel scene was brought out by the majority of students. They were then given further opportunities for practice by analysing the following extracts so as to detect climaxes. These scenes in whole or in part were then rehearsed by the students. They can be treated as supplementary exercises.

Exercise 1. Mrs. Warren's Profession—Bernard Shaw *(Act IV).*

The sequence between Mrs. Warren and her daughter Vivie, starting with—

Vivie: No: I am my mother's daughter . . . and continuing til the end of the play.

Exercise 2. The Seagull (Anton Chekhov)
    Act III Arkadina and Treplev
    Act III Arkadina and Trigorin

Exercise 3. *Pygmalion* (Bernard Shaw).
       Act IV Higgins and Eliza.

Only short sequences from the above scenes should be attempted with beginners. Later the whole scenes can be rehearsed.

Other excerpts of a similar nature are:

    Othello (William Shakespeare)

    Act V. Sc. 2. Othello and Emilia.

    Emilia: Oh my good Lord, yonder's foul murder done . . . and continuing to—

    Emilia: The Moor hath killed my mistress. Murder, murder!

    Hamlet (William Shakespeare)

    Act III. Sc. 4. Hamlet and the Queen. Polonius hidden behind a curtain.

    Hamlet: Now mother, what's the matter? . . . and continuing till the end of the scene.

    Measure for Measure (William Shakespeare)

    Act III. Sc. 1. Isabella and Claudio.

    Isabella: Be ready, Claudio, for your death tomorrow . . . up to—

    Claudio: Oh hear me Isabella.

It will be found that once the student grasps the principle of building up to the climax and the tension point followed by the relaxation of tension the necessary variation in the voice follows. The impetus of the scene when it gets under way helps to ensure the necessary pace.

The use of approaching moves in the build-up of a quarrel followed by a relaxing move as it subsides, has an interesting parallel in the build up to a laugh line in comedy acting. (see page 111).

SUMMARY

1. When rehearsing quarrel sequences the actor and producer must first discover the reason for the quarrel and the underlying rhythm.

2. Major and minor climaxes must be detected.

3. The action usually builds up to its climax which is followed by a pause (tension point). The tension is then usually relieved by a relaxed move and a quieter delivery of the lines.

4. Prolonged quarrel scenes may contain several minor climaxes leading up to a major one as in the Brutus-Cassius scene from *Julius Caesar*.

5. Prolonged shouting can destroy the desired effect and irritate the audience.

6. Each performer must give himself a definite purpose for his part in the quarrel.

7. Experiment 5 gives an example of such a sequence in which the pattern has been detected.

★ 7 ★

Creating Mood and Atmosphere

FROM time to time we meet those magical scenes when a whole mood, nostalgic, uncanny or exciting takes possession of the characters in a play and succeeds in captivating the audience. Such was often my experience when carrying out experiments on emotion memory (see page 56). With crowd scenes the creation of such moods is more difficult, for if only one performer is out of key with the rest, the thread is broken and the illusion destroyed. The plays of Chekhov abound in instances of scenes of mood. The extract from *The Seagull* is an excellent example. In such cases it is essential that the directions be given in the pervading mood, so that the students do not have to adjust themselves from, say, the cold efficient tones of a producer, to the atmosphere of nostalgia of the text. Crime and horror plays are another case in point. They require very careful handling and the actors must convey that sense of fear and tension which accompanies the unknown. Similarly, in turbulent scenes of battle all the combatants must convey the air of excitement, and if necessary interpret the changing fortunes of war; elation following despair or vice versa, as in many a Shakespearian History.

EXPERIMENT 6. AIM: TO CREATE ATMOSPHERE IN
A SCENE OF MOOD

Number involved: 3 women. 5 men.

The following extract from Act One of *The Seagull* by Anton Chekhov, is to be studied by the performers.

The Characters.

Arkadina   — an actress.
Trigorin   — a writer, her lover.
Sorin   — her brother.
Shamrayeff   — a retired Army lieutenant, Sorin's bailiff.
Polena   — his wife.
Masha   — his daughter.
Dorn   — a doctor.
Medviedenko   — a schoolmaster.

The Scene.

The park on Sorin's estate. A wide avenue leads towards a lake in the background. A rough stage erected for an amateur theatrical performance has been built across the avenue and conceals the view of the lake. There are bushes close to the stage, and in the foreground a few chairs and a bench. The sun is setting.

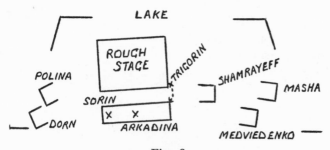

Fig. 6
Plan of Set:

The Situation.

Arkadina has offended her son Constantine by poking fun at his play, and he has left the assembled company in anger and disgust. After the discomfiture that this has caused, they now settle down to enjoy the evening.

The Text.

Arkadina. . . . . But don't let us talk about plays now. It's such a
        beautiful evening . . . Listen everybody . . . Is that
        somebody singing? . . .
        (they listen)
        How lovely!
Polina.   It's on the other side.
        (a pause).
Arkadina. (to Trigorin) Sit down here, by me. Ten or fifteen
        years ago music and singing were heard on the lake
        nearly every night. There were six houses round the
        lake. I can still remember the laughter, the noise
        and the shooting—and love affairs, those love affairs!
        The matinee idol of the six houses was—let me intro-
        duce him (nodding towards Dorn) Dr. Eugene
        Sergeyitch. Even now he's fascinating, but then he
        was irresistible. But my conscience is beginning to
        prick me. Why did I hurt my poor boy? I'm really
        worried. Kostya! Son! Kostya!
Masha.   I'll go and look for him.
Arkadina. Please do, dear.
Masha.   Ay-oo——Constantine Gavrilovitch . . . Ay-oo——
        (she exits left)

Directions given.

At the beginning of the scene your positions are as on the plan.
(see page 71).

Imagine that it is a close summer night and most of you are
already feeling drowsy. The music you hear is a peasant song
which echoes from the other side of the lake.

Masha is looking towards the LEFT where Constantine, whom
she loves, has gone off. She is lost in thought, sympathising with
him in his sense of failure and despair.

Medviedenko, her suitor, is thinking of the miserable life he leads as a schoolmaster who supports the rest of his family.

Trigorin at the beginning of the scene is half listening to Medviedenko and enjoying the view of the lake. Being a professional writer, he is mentally trying to put his impressions into words. His thoughts are interrupted by Arkadina asking him to sit by her.

Sorin who is quite fond of his nephew is glad that the boy's quarrel with his mother is over. He sits dreaming of the life he himself might have led had fate been kinder to him.

Arkadina is being nostalgic as she recalls the romantic past and sets the mood of the scene.

Dorn, the former man about town, is flattered by Arkadina's compliments.

Polena who is very much in love with Dorn, cannot keep her eyes off him. She is jealous, perhaps, of Arkadina's show of admiration for him.

Shamrayeff, the complete egoist, is enjoying the music and is hardly aware of the others.

Everybody is seated except Masha and Trigorin. The latter turns towards the others to make a note of something during the pause, when he catches Arkadina's eye and she invites him to join her.

Arkadina rises on, "But my conscience is beginning to prick me", thereby breaking the mood. She walks U.L. crossing beyond Masha as she calls "Kostya!" Masha offers to go and look for him. As she leaves, her calls must have a sense of echo to fit in with the prevailing lyrical mood.

Notes:

1. The scene was run through several times.
2. For the purpose of the exercise the song off-stage had to be imagined by the students. Later an old Russian Folk Song was hummed to give the effect of distant singing.

Comments.

The students were not slow to capture the prevailing mood of lethargy and nostalgia. This was especially evident during the long pause which followed "Is that somebody singing?" Even in the first rendering the words, "How lovely!" and, "It's on the other side of the lake", were spoken as if the actresses concerned were enjoying the music in idyllic surroundings. Much depended on the actress playing Arkadina. Two different performances are worthy of description. In the first the actress delivered her lines langorously, savouring her own description of the happy past. She interrupted this by an obviously insincere reference to her conscience when she realised that Trigorin was not terribly interested. In the second rendering the Arkadina was a little more animated in her picture of the days gone by and looked rather coaxingly at Dorn as she spoke of him—she interrupted herself when she realised that this might be offending Trigorin.

Errors.

1. Students not endowed with a good sense of theatre did not hold the pauses long enough, thus breaking the effect of leisureliness. (The Russians are adept at holding long pauses and in the original production by Stanislavsky pauses of 10 or more seconds were not uncommon). This error was often the starting point for giving the students instruction and practice in the use of pauses on general. The solution in this particular case was for the performer to think of as many things as possible relevant to the stage situation during the pause and to break it only when prolongation would either produce a rather comic effect or give the impression that there had been a "dry". Only once did this latter fault occur, the actress in question being over anxious not to give the impression of haste.

2. Students who, having no words to speak, were not really participating. This very rarely occurred, owing to the care taken in giving the initial directions with the suggested thoughts

of all the characters. When it did occur it was usually because either (i) the student did not agree with my suggestions, in which case he was asked to think of alternatives in keeping with the general tenor of the scene; or (ii) because he was too aware of the audience and thus not sufficiently absorbed in the role. If this was the case he was given several definite objects on the lake or in the park on which to focus his attention. Each object was to remind him of an incident in that happy past which Arkadina was alluding to. (Compare this with the exercise on emotion memory).

3. Reciting the lines. Again this did not often occur. When it did I would re-state the mood of the scene and ask the student to deliver a few lines in the right key, so to speak. This was generally successful and the method later proved useful in helping an artist whose conception of a part was totally at variance with the author's and producer's intention. By getting one part of the performance in the right key, the rest will often automatically fall into place, providing that the student is willing to tackle the rest of the part according to the already mastered interpretation of the 'key' passage. It is a very useful method when there is only a limited amount of time for individual rehearsal.

Supplementary Exercises.

1. *The Three Sisters.* Anton Chekhov. (*Act I, Sc.* 1).

Olga. Father died just a year ago today—your Saint's day, Irina. It was very cold then, and it was snowing. I felt that I should never get over it and you were lying there in a faint, quite still, as though you were dead. Now a year's gone by and here we are, talking about it quite calmly. You're dressed in white and your face is radiant.
(the clock strikes twelve)
Yes, the clock was striking twelve then too. (a pause). I remember that when father was carried to the cemetery the band was playing and a rifle salute was fired. He was

a general, the commander of the brigade and yet there
weren't many people there. But then it was raining.
Raining and snowing hard.

Here Olga is in a reminiscent mood, comparing that bleak
day with the happy one which is the occasion of Irina's birthday.
The speech must not be made gloomy.

2. *The Cherry Orchard*. Anton Chekhov. (*Act II*).
   The whole of this Act repays study from the point of view of
mood music, of which Chekhov was master.

3. *A Midsummer Night's Dream*. William Shakespeare.
Oberon.   Thou rememb'rest
   Since once I sat upon a promontory,
   And heard a mermaid on a dolphin's back
   Uttering such dulcet and harmonious breath,
   That the rude sea grew civil at her song,
   And certain stars shot madly from their spheres,
   To hear the sea-maid's music.
Puck. I remember.

The listening attitude of Puck is important. The best performance of this sequence I have seen was when Puck sat en-
raptured by the beauty of the words and the music described and
exaltedly whispered, "I remember".

4. *A Haunted House*. An exercise for three students.
   You are visiting a house which is reputed to be haunted. Stop
dead still as you think you hear strange sounds. React to sights
that are out of the ordinary. The mood to be created is one of
mystery and fear.

5. A change of mood from joy to sadness. (Five performers).
   One student enters the room feeling very happy as a result of
having passed his examinations. The others are despondent for
they have failed. The general atmosphere of gloom checks his

feeling of elation. He pauses for a short while and, without saying a word, makes his exit.

Plays which contain further examples are:

Little Lambs Eat Ivy. Noel Langley.

An expectant father is awaiting the birth of a baby. Choose any passage from this play which illustrates the mood of anxious waiting.

A Day by the Sea. N. C. Hunter.

A modern play in a Chekhovian setting and atmosphere.

The Diary of Anne Frank. F. Goodrich and A. Hackett.

Throughout this play there is an atmosphere of tension. At any moment the group of Jews hidden in a loft may be discovered by the Gestapo. The final discovery by the enemy is almost a relief although they know that death will be the inevitable result.

SUMMARY

The mood or atmosphere of a sequence, i.e. whether it is lethargic, mysterious, exciting or nostalgic, must be conveyed to the audience by sensitive team acting.

1. It is best to rehearse in the prevailing mood of the play.
2. Pauses charged with inner meaning can help to engender the correct mood.
3. In cases of difficulty it helps to repeat one or two lines or a whole speech according to the key mood of the sequence. The rest of the scene will often fall into line.
4. Exercises containing examples of scenes of different types of moods are described.

Hidden Meaning and Charged Dialogue.

WORDS sometimes say one thing and mean another. It is the challenge of the written word that its surface meaning is often a cloak for something of deeper significance. To the actor this can present a real difficulty. He must first discover what the author really *meant* and not just what he *said*. In *Macbeth* the words (spoken by Macbeth), "Duncan comes here tonight" do not just announce the arrival of an honoured guest. They signify more than that—perhaps, "Here's an opportunity to get rid of him". Similarly, when Hamlet asks Ophelia, "Where's your father?" he has already realised that the father, Polonius, is listening to their conversation and so the words have a deeper significance. Again, when Othello almost casually asks Desdemona for the handkerchief, he believes that her failure to produce it will be positive proof of her infidelity. The tritest statement, the most inane remark, must be spoken so as to bring out the wealth of meaning that lies beneath it, if such is the author's intention.

Sometimes the student finds this task of conveying the author's hidden meaning rather difficult. A slavish copy of the producer's rendering of the word or phrase is frequently of no avail in bringing the performance to life, because it is after all merely a surface copy. He can be helped by being taught to point or stress important words, to vary the pitch of his voice or to suspend the action of a piece of business (see page 96) but these mechanical aids are also frequently found to be inadequate. The solution lies in thinking or feeling right rather than in the correct surface delivery of the words. I have found the method described in Experiment 7 to be the most successful one. The student is given words to think while he speaks the text. The extract chosen illustrates Noel Coward's skill in the employment of this charged dialogue.

There are many interesting variations of this method which can be of great assistance in solving problems not specifically concerned with charged dialogue. In the preliminary study of Shakespearian speeches, for instance, many of the more obscure passages can be made real and comprehensible to the performer by a judicious paraphrase which captures the spirit of the original. It is often the teacher's task to do this. The student, having grasped the meaning, can now tackle the text with more confidence and with increased chances of success. Again, there are many instances when an actor has to play against the main line of his part; for example when it is necessary to show the lighter shades of what is essentially a serious role. The method then employed is to ask the student to make up dialogue in a lighter vein than the original, and to carry in his mind this improvised dialogue while speaking the text.

EXPERIMENT 7.

Number involved: One man. One woman.

The following extract from Noel Coward's *Still Life*, is to be given to the students for close study, after they have read the complete play.

The Characters.

Laura Jesson — a pleasant, ordinary married woman.

Alec Harvey — a doctor.

The Scene.

The Refreshment room of Milford Junction Station. For the purpose of this exercise the scene is set as follows:

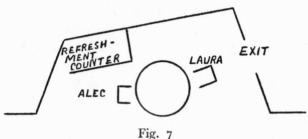

Fig. 7

The Situation.

Alec and Laura, both happily married, and with respectable middle-class backgrounds, first met each other in this station buffet, when Alec removed a piece of grit from Laura's eye. After one or two chance meetings it is becoming obvious to them both that they are falling in love with each other. Here Alec is telling her of his ideals and aspirations as a doctor.

The Text.

Alec.   What I mean is this—all good doctors must be primarily enthusiasts. They must have, like writers and painters and priests, a sense of vocation—a deep-rooted, unsentimental desire to do good.

Laura. Yes I see that.

Alec.   Well, obviously one way of preventing disease is worth fifty ways of curing it—that's where my ideal comes in— preventive medicine isn't anything to do with medicine at all, really—it's concerned with conditions, living conditions and common-sense and hygiene. For instance, my speciality is pneumoconiosis.

Laura. Oh, dear!

Alec.   Don't be alarmed, it's simpler than it sounds—it's nothing but a slow fibrosis of the lung due to the inhalation of particles of dust. In the hospital there are splendid opportunities for observing cures and making notes, because of the coal mines.

Laura. You suddenly look much younger.

Alec. (Brought up short). Do I?

Laura. Almost like a little boy.

Alec. What made you say that?

Laura. (staring at him) I don't know—yes I do.

Alec. (gently) Tell me.

Laura. (with panic in her voice) Oh, no —I couldn't really. You were saying about the coal mines . . .

Alec. (looking into her eyes) Yes:—the inhalation of coal dust . . . that's one specific form of the disease . . . it's called anthracosis.

Laura. (hypnotised) What are the others?

Alec. Chalicosis—that comes from metal dust—steel works, you know . . .

Laura. Yes, of course. Steel works.

Alec. And silicosis—stone dust—that's gold mines.

Laura. (almost in a whisper) I see.

(there is the sound of a bell)

Directions given.

To *Alec:* You are full of enthusiasm as you speak on your pet subject. For a time you are lost in your account of it. You are pulled up sharply by her cutting across what you are saying with the sudden remark, "You suddenly look much younger". It is this that brings you back to complete awareness of her. You want her to come out into the open and tell you that she loves you, for you now realise that this is the case. Throughout your following speeches you must try and say it with your eyes.

To *Laura:* At first listen to his words with interest. As he becomes more and more absorbed in his subject, say to yourself, "How boyish and enthusiastic he looks—how attractive and lovable he is". Your first two interjections—"Yes, I see that" and

"Oh, dear" barely interrupt his train of thought. When you say, "You suddenly look much younger" and, "Almost like a little boy", you are blurting out what you think. It is when Alec asks you why, that you realise it is because you are very much attracted to him. You are afraid of bringing this into the open, hence the panic and your desperate attempts to change the subject.

After this you are wholly taken up with each other, as though in a trance. The surface words mean very little; underneath them there is the tension which prevails before the lovers declare their love for each other. Therefore *try and think* the following dialogue, or something like it, during the sequence which begins with Alec looking into her eyes and saying, "Yes—the inhalation of coal dust . . . that's one specific form of the disease", and ending with Laura's whispered, "I see".

Alec. I love you.
Laura. Yes, I know.
Alec. But I can't bring myself to tell you.
Laura. I know that too.

Repeat this sequence of dialogue in your minds so that it roughly covers the time that it takes to speak the written dialogue of the text.

The tension is mercifully broken by the sound of the station bell that signals the approach of Alec's train.

Notes.
1. It was found that by actually playing the sequence using my improvised dialogue and then repeating it using the correct version, pupils had no subsequent difficulty in thinking and feeling along the right lines as they played the scene.

2. The performance was repeated several times until the students were at home in it.

Comments.

1. This method was reasonably successful with students of varying degrees of ability. I had already tried to help them by giving 'correct' intonations and emphasis but without much success, because even when they did not find it difficult to copy me, their interpretations were entirely on the surface and did not ring true.

2. Following this experiment. I used other suitable material in which a similar method of dealing with charged dialogue could be employed. Both Coward and Rattigan are masters of this type of writing, and there are scenes from *The Browning Version* and from *Private Lives* which are good examples of it. In the latter the problem of maintaining the balance between surface humour and underlying romantic seriousness is a fascinating one, particularly in the balcony scene between Ellyot and Amanda in Act I.

Errors.

1. Overpointing with unnecessary pauses, making the scene too heavy. This was a common fault, particularly in the actors who played the role of Alec. By giving those who made this mistake plenty of practice in throwing away lines, much was done to eradicate this. A slow, over-laboured delivery was often due to bad control of breathing and was dealt with in the Speech Training Course.

2. Hurrying through the latter part of the scene. This did not often occur when the method described above was correctly employed. It usually disappeared on the second run through of the scene when pointed out to the offender.

Supplementary Exercises.

1. *A prison scene:*

Joan is visiting her brother who is in prison for murder.
Joan. It's been raining all day.

Tom. I haven't noticed—in here. I've been on library duty. I gave up my exercise. Special dispensation, I suppose.

Joan. Am I allowed to give you a cigarette?

Tom. (Looks at the warder and smiles) I shouldn't think so for a moment.

(a pause. Then she plucks up courage to speak again)

Joan. (softly) Why did you do it, dear?

Tom. Must I answer that?

Both performers are to improvise dialogue which they are to think during the speaking of trivialities which lead up to Joan's question, "Why did you do it, dear?" During the pause Joan is bracing herself to ask the question which has been tormenting her. The scene can be continued as an exercise in improvisation.

2. Archie Rice has just heard that his son has been taken prisoner by the Japanese. In order to cheer himself up he tells his daughter a funny story. On the surface he is cheerful, but underneath he is full of misery and despair. Imagine that you are Archie—tell a story of your own choosing and interrupt yourself when you can no longer keep up the pretence. Now compare your version with the final sequence of Act I, of *The Entertainer* by John Osborne.

3. Alice meets Peter from whom she has been parted for several years. They have just seen each other at a fair-ground. While in the course of exchanging several light banalities they discover that they are still in love with each other.

Alice. Look at that funny little man at the coconut shy.

Peter. He doesn't seem to be having much luck.

Alice. They're playing the same old tune on the roundabout. Look!—there's that fat man helping his wife on to one of the horses.

Peter. I did that to you once.

Alice. You weren't quite so fat.

Peter. You weren't quite so heavy.

Alice. He's strong too.

Peter. (looking at her) That at least hasn't altered.

Improvise the underlying dialogue for this scene and then rehearse it.

Compare it with Act I scene I of *Private Lives* by Noel Coward in which Amanda meets Ellyot after a long parting. The sequence ends with Ellyot saying, "Unbelievable, a sort of dream".

4. From *Three Sisters*. Anton Chekhov.

Act IV. Irina and *Tuzenbach*.

Tuzenbach is going off to fight a duel unbeknown to Irina to whom he is engaged.

Tuzenbach. (kissing her hand) Goodbye my darling. The papers which you gave me are on my table under the calendar.

Irina. I'll come with you.

Tuzenbach. (in agitation) No, no! (he goes off quickly then turns back in the avenue) Irina!

Irina. What?

Tuzenbach. (not knowing what to say) I haven't had any coffee to-day. Tell them to make me some. (He exits quickly).

Tuzenbach goes to his death. He was on the point of saying something important to Irina. Before you play this scene try to decide what he wanted to say.

SUMMARY

1. The words of the playwright can have a deeper (or implied) meaning than the one they appear to possess on the surface. This true meaning must be discovered by the performer and conveyed to the audience.

2. To do this successfully he must think and feel correctly rather than slavishly copy the producer's intonations.

3. The actor should himself think what the character might be thinking while uttering the dialogue of the text. This is explained and practised in Experiment 7.

4. Mentally paraphrasing an obscure text can often reveal its real meaning and help the student to acquire the correct intonation.

5. When the lighter shades of an essentially serious role are to be portrayed it is advisable to improvise dialogue in a lighter vein while studying the part.

6. Similarly when studying the serious facets of an essentially amusing or light-hearted role it helps to improvise dialogue of a serious nature.

⋆ 9 ⋆

Good and Bad Timing

TIMING in the theatre has been a bone of contention for many years. "What do you mean by good timing?" asks many a student actor. The answer is, "Go and watch a really good performance. See how the artist does exactly the right thing at the right time so as to have the desired effect on the audience, how he uses all the means at his disposal without awkwardness or fuss—you will then be seeing good timing in action". Bad timing on the other hand is like bad ballroom dancing—if you do not co-ordinate your steps with that of your partner, you will tread on her toes. In acting, that partner is the audience.

Timing embraces every part of theatrical training: modulation of the voice, the use of pauses, the use of movement and gesture, the making of entrances and exits. It is only when the student becomes adept in co-ordinating these aspects in his performance that he becomes an exponent of good timing—and a competent artist.

Here are examples of good timing: Sir Laurence Olivier's first entrance in Bernard Shaw's *Caesar and Cleopatra*. He entered quietly out of the gloom, a frail figure, and stood still, almost visibly growing in stature as he began to address the Sphinx. The audience were entranced. Then Dame Edith Evan's unexpected breaking into song in James Bridie's *Daphne Laureola* can be instanced as another example of perfect timing. That great actress seemed to choose the exact moment to surprise and delight

87

the spectator. Again Sir Ralph Richardson's turning of the latch key in the lock as he came back home after a twenty-four hour's absence in R. C. Sherrif's *Home at Seven*, deliberately belied the tense situation which that absence had already created. By the minimum of effort the actor suggested that an office worker was returning home at the usual time and was ready for his evening meal.

In Arthur Miller's *The Crucible* John Proctor is asked by the Reverend John Hale to recite the Ten Commandments in order to prove that he is a good Christian and not tainted with witchcraft. Hale neither knows or suspects that Proctor has committed adultery. Proctor begins slowly and then quickens the pace as he gains confidence, even though he is not reciting the Commandments in their correct order. He hestitates as he comes to the seventh which concerns adultery. After a short pause his wife prompts him.

Now it is this pause before his wife speaks which can make or mar the performance. If it is too long the thread is broken and the action of the play sags. If it is not long enough the irony of the situation is missed. The whole of this sequence requires a good sense of timing from the three performers and should be studied with this aspect in mind.

Can good timing be taught? Many teachers say it cannot. It *can*, just as ballroom dancing can be taught, providing that the student has a minimum basic sense of rhythm. In movement and speech classes he is often helped to acquire this.

This experiment is concerned with the co-ordination of speech, movement and the handling of a stage property.

EXPERIMENT 10.

Number involved: One student.

The Set: One chair is set up stage centre.

Stage 1.

Directions given before and after demonstration.

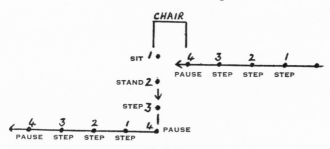

Fig. 8
Diagram illustrating Stage 1
The beat is 4/4 time.
During the pause on beat 4 bring the rear foot to front foot.

You are to approach the chair from the left in time to the beat which is tapped out to you; when you come on a level with the chair, pause, sit, then rise and take one step forward—still in time to the beat: then turn and take three steps to the right—again in time to the beat. The instructor will demonstrate it to you.

Stage 2.

Directions given.

Repeat the movement as for Stage 1 with the addition of this piece of dialogue.

1. "I couldn't care less".

Say this as you walk towards the chair, then sit immediately you finish the last word as if to clinch the matter. (The imagined answer is "That's just like you").

2. "So that's what you think".

Say this agressively as you rise and take a step forward.

3. "Oh, well, I might have known".

Shrug your shoulders and walk the three steps to the left as you say this.

The sequence is repeated two or three times.

Stage 3.

Directions given.

Repeat the above with the addition of the following piece of stage business.

1. On the words, "So that's what you think", take out a revolver from your pocket and point it menacingly at your imaginary stage partner.

2. As you say, "Oh, well, I might have known", put the revolver away again and co-ordinate this with your three steps away to the left.

This is repeated until there is smooth co-ordination between steps, words and the handling of the revolver according to directions given.

Comments.

By commencing with a regular rhythmic beat and a set pattern of movement the student was led to discover his own individual rhythm; only then was the exercise repeated with the inclusion of speech and stage business. Constant repetition was found to be necessary for those who found this difficult. It must be pointed out that no specific situation was given. This was to be considered a mechanical exercise, and it was the framework which was important, i.e. the three initial steps, the halt, sitting down and rising, etc. These are constant factors such as exist on a stage with a limited amount of acting space.

Errors.

1. Inability to keep to the rhythmic beat in Stage 1. This was cured by repetition of the exercise until the student had mastered the rhythm.

2. Lack of co-ordination between the steps and words; either the speech and the steps were in two different rhythms or there was overlapping of the speech when the movement had stopped.

3. Awkwardness or fussiness in the handling of the revolver. This was tackled by treating it as a drill movement, the movement being done by numbers. Exercises such as those described in the handling of properties (pages 96 and 99) also proved useful.

The exercises, modified according to the needs of individual groups, were used in the Movement Class.

Supplementary Exercises.

1. *Making an Entrance. King Henry IV. Part I.*

King Henry enters with his attendant noblemen and addresses them.

King Henry. So shaken as we are, so wan with care,
　　　　　Find we a time for frighted peace to pant,
　　　　　And breathe short-winded accents of new broils
　　　　　To be commenced in stronds afar remote.

Make your entrance as the King. Mount the four steps of the rostrum, turn, hold a pause and begin the speech.

The rest of the class are to act as an audience and to judge whether the whole of this sequence is well or badly timed.

2. *Titania's Entrance. A Midsummer-Night's Dream (Act II, Sc. 1).*

Enter Oberon on one side with his train, and Titania from the other, with hers.

Oberon. Ill met by moonlight, proud Titania.

Titania. What! Jealous Oberon.

Let Oberon enter first from stage Right and then Titania from Up Stage Centre. Both must time their halts and any pauses before speaking.

3. *Hamlet's entrance in the closet scene. Hamlet (Act III, Sc. 4).*

He should enter as though in haste and then pause before he says, "Now mother, what's the matter?" The timing of this entrance should be checked by the instructor.

4. *The timing of a gesture.*

This must be prompted from within and is dependent on the character portrayed and on the author's text.

Here is an example, again from *Hamlet*, this time from the battlement scene.

Marcellus. Peace! break thee off; look where it comes again!
     (Enter Ghost)
Bernardo. In the same figure, like the king that's dead.

Imagine that you are Marcellus and point towards the vague figure of the ghost as it appears out of the shadows. The rest of the class is to judge whether the pointing at the ghost is correctly timed.

5. *Walking About.*

Imagine you are Dunois at the beginning of Scene Three of *St. Joan* by George Bernard Shaw. Walk about as you mutter your curses at the West wind. Dunois cannot attack the English positions until the wind rises and allows his men to sail towards them. He is cursing it for not complying with his wishes.

Determine when you will halt and when you will pace up and down in silence. Shaw's stage directions should be carefully studied before you begin this exercise. Remember to work yourself up to the rhythm of impatience before you start to talk. This can be done by pacing about for some time in silence while you imagine this frustrating situation until you feel you cannot remain silent any longer.

6. *The exit of Malvolio.* (*Twelfth Night. Act V. Sc.* 1).

Malvolio is furious when he learns that he has been tricked by the clown and the other revellers into believing that Olivia is in love with him. His last words as he leaves are, "I'll be revenged on the whole pack of you".

Make this exit. Determine whether he says these words before he moves or during his exit.

7. *The Exit of Letitia. The Belle's Stratagem* by Hannah Cowley. (*Act I, Sc.* 3).

Letitia is planning a ruse to attract Doricourt her fiancé, who has been indifferent to her charms. Her father, Mr. Hardy—and her friend, Mrs. Racket are listening to her plan.

Letitia. Why sir—it may seem a little paradoxical—but as he does not like me enough, I want him to like me still less; and will, at our next interview, endeavour to heighten his indifference into dislike.

Hardy. Who the devil could have foreseen that?

Mrs. Racket. Heaven and earth! Letitia, are you serious?

Letitia. As serious as the most important business of my life demands.

Mrs. Racket. Why endeavour to make him dislike you?

Letitia. Because 'tis much easier to convert a sentiment into its opposite, than to transform indifference into tender passion.

Mrs. Racket. That may be good philosophy, but I'm afraid you'll find it a bad maxim.

Letitia. I have the strongest confidence in it. I am inspired with unusual spirits; and on this hazard, willingly stake my chance for happiness. I am impatient to begin my measures. (Exit).

Here Letitia is as she says impatient to set to work to allure Doricourt. Thus the exit must be a hurried one. The actress must decide whether she is to exit as she says, "I am impatient to begin my measures", or whether she should say her line first, and then make her exit. Both can be correct depending on the personal timing of the person playing the role.

Several students in the class can perform this while the others judge whether the timing is correct for the person concerned.

SUMMARY

1. *Good timing* means taking the appropriate action in speech, movement or gesture, so as to have the desired effect on the audience.

2. *Bad timing* occurs when this action is not taken at the right moment and the desired effect misfires.

3. Timing enters into all branches of training. Actors must learn to time their entrances, exits, delivery of lines, handling of properties and any other stage business.

4. Good timing depends on the possession of a basic sense of rhythm. Providing that this is present it can be learnt.

5. Good timing can be taught using mechanical means such as those employed in Experiment 8.

★ 10 ★

Handling Stage Properties

EARLY in rehearsals the actor ought to be provided with the properties he will require for the actual performance. Failing this, substitutes should be found which are sufficiently close to the originals to ensure that essential stage business is not omitted. We see too often a hand sawing the air instead of holding a stick, book or cigarette, the result being that at a later stage the process of co-ordinating speech and stage business becomes doubly difficult.

The following points should be borne in mind when training the student to handle properties correctly:

1. Accuracy. To take an obvious example, a heavy trunk should not be lifted as though it were a light suitcase; and a less obvious one, a glass of wine should not be tasted as though it were a cup of tea. Miming the desired action is a useful preliminary and often ensures accuracy. It should be followed by practice with the object itself.

2. The flow of action of the play must not be interrupted by the use of properties unless this is specifically required by the author or producer. In a badly acted sequence one often notices that the flow of performance stops as we wait for the actor to put on his coat or light the ubiquitous cigarette. This dead pause makes no positive contribution to the play. It is a vacuum during which the action sags.

When stage business does not emphasise something connected with the plot, it should either be cut out or co-ordinated with the dialogue so as to be unobtrusive.

3. Conversely, when the action calls for it, the flow of a sequence can be halted by deliberately "freezing" the handling of a property. Examples of this are when one wants to point a line or to register a reaction. Sudden stillness has just this effect. An appropriate example is when Freddie in Rattigan's *The Deep Blue Sea* suspends the action of pouring out a drink for his friend by standing still, bottle in hand. In this way he points his next line, "She tried to kill herself last night". The line is given additional importance instead of being lost in the flow of dialogue. There are also numerous examples in Noel Coward's *Still Life* where the act of drinking a cup of tea or eating a bun, when interrupted, can be charged with special significance.

This experiment, incorporating the above points, was employed in order to find a method of giving instruction and practice in the handling of properties.

EXPERIMENT 9. AIM: TO LEARN HOW TO HANDLE PROPERTIES

Directions given:

Stage 1. Mime the following actions.

    i. Take a cigarette case out of your pocket (or handbag).

    ii. Extract the cigarette and light it with a lighter which is also to be found in your pocket (or handbag).

    Do this as one continuous action.

    Try to visualise the correct sequence.

Stage 2. Repeat the above exercise with the actual objects.

Stage 3. Repeat this sequence with the objects, at the same time fitting in the words "It's nice to see you again", so that there is no hold up in either the movement or the delivery of the words. Do this several times until you feel that the words and the action are smooth and co-ordinated.

Stage 4. Repeat the above, this time imagining that your partner has said something that has shocked you (e.g. "You're a liar") and find one place where you can stop (suspend) the action so that your reaction is emphasized.

Stage 5. Think of as many places as possible in the action where you could interrupt and suspend the movement so as to point a line or heighten your reaction to something or somebody.

Now repeat the above exercise trying out some of these stopping points.

Comments.

1. The miming in Stage 1 did help with the actual handling of the cigarette case, cigarette and cigarette lighter, and ensured that the correct sequence was followed without fussiness and awkwardness. It also helped with the acquisition of correct timing when the words were added in Stage 3.

2. Later when the action was interrupted to point the line (Stage 4) several unsuccessful attempts were made by most performers before they found the most effective spot to pause. In some cases I repeated this part of the experiment with an audience of students who were to choose which halting point in the performance was the most effective. It was then found that these points varied from person to person. The exercise was thus useful as an introduction to students of the concept of personal or individual timing, i.e. that two people may do quite different things and yet be equally effective, because the action co-ordinates with their own natural rhythm of movement, speech, etc.

3. In Stage 5 the number of interruption points found in practice was a revelation to the students. As many as twenty were revealed in this simple action alone. Some of these are listed here:

    a.   When feeling in the pocket for the lighter.
    b.   As the case is being lifted.
    c.   As the case is opened.
    d.   When the cigarette is extracted.
    e.   As the cigarette is being lifted.
    f.   When the case is put away.
    g.   As the lighter is found.
    h.   When the lighter is brought out.
    i.   Just before the flick of the lighter.
    j.   As the cigarette is lighted.

After Stage 5 I usually made the student repeat Stage 3—the continuous smooth action—so that he should not become over-conscious of the individual movements; if this is not done the outcome might be a hesitant performance.

The total result of the experiment was that the student, by analysis and practice of simple movements involving the use of properties, gained more control of the specialised 'timed' move-ment and gestures which are so essential to the finished per-formance. I was once privileged to watch a rehearsal taken by that excellent producer Mr. Peter Glenville in which the lighting of a cigarette and a few subsequent words were rehearsed at least a dozen times before the desired effect was obtained. To me it was an object lesson in the care and attention a would-be actor must pay to the detailed work involved in even the simplest actions.

Common Errors.

1. Telescoping i.e. missing out links in the chain of action. For instance in the mime several students forgot to flick the lighter or to put away the cigarette case. When this happened I insisted

that the action be repeated at first slowly and then faster until the complete sequence became second nature.

2. In Stage 4 there was a tendency to forget to complete the movement after the pause, so that the cigarette case, cigarette or lighter was held in the air too long. A pause must be followed by a relaxing move to relieve the tension (compare this with a quarrel sequence). The order of movement should be:

   i.   begin the action

   ii. interrupt the action as you react to the words, "you're a liar"

   iii. Complete the action at a different pace according to the change of mood which follows the pause.

Supplementary Exercises.

1. Unfold a newspaper, read the headlines, then fold it up again and put it away. Interrupt the action when somebody speaks to you.

2. Find the right key in the bunch you are carrying and unlock the door. Find the interruption points in the action.

3. Mime cleaning your shoes, then find possible interruption points.

4. Practice opening and shutting a door in varying situations, e.g. an escape, after a parting, visiting an old friend.

5. Repeat the experiment using the following actions:

Drinking a cup of tea, eating a meal, pouring out drinks, bandaging a wound, using the telephone.

SUMMARY

   1.   Properties or substitute properties should be provided early in rehearsals so as to give the actor sufficient practice in handling them.

2. When using properties the performer should aim at
   a. being accurate
   b. not holding up the flow of action of the play, unless this is planned as a deliberate effect.
3. Pausing while handling a property is a useful device for pointing a line or for registering a reaction.
4. Miming the action, at the same time trying to recall the correct sequence, helps to ensure accuracy. This is used in Experiment 9.
5. Exercises in suspended (interrupted) movement help the actor to establish control over the handling of properties.

Acting in Comedy

LAUGHTER in the theatre is much more predictable than is commonly imagined. In spite of the variable conditions under which a performance takes place, such as the type of audience and the particular brand of wit or humour in the text, the skilful producer of Comedy can plan for his laughter reaction from the audience. This entails mastering the general principles and the tricks of comedy. Incongruities, sharp contrasts, repetition are included in these. In that excellent book *The Craft of Comedy* Miss Athene Seyler says that the essentials of Comedy Acting are—

"lack of balance, distortion, over-emphasis or under-emphasis, and surprise. Now all these things are relative to something else: the truth. So that you must first see the truth of a character before you can upset its balance. But you must *believe* in the distorted view of the truth that you have discovered. Having drawn the character a little out of proportion you must passionately believe in that measurement as the correct one. I think that your true comedian does both these things at once; that is to say, he is aware instinctively that the emphasis he is laying on one side of his portrait distorts it, and yet he offers it as a true likeness. The 'standing outside'—the approach to the character—is the first process. The second process is concerned with presenting this view, and depends on what we call technique. It is the craft of appearing to believe in the balance of a thing that one knows to be out of balance. That sounds like a theory of tight-rope walking! And indeed I think it is mental tight-rope walking in which the slightest slip ends in disaster. If you forget the whole character while presenting one angle, or you lose your vivid consciousness of this angle in your realisation of the other sides of the character, your intention with regard to the audience will be lost."

Thus the comic actor should go through three stages when studying his role—

1.   He must view the character from a distance, seeing it in perspective.
2.   He selects one side of the character and emphasises it.
3.   He must then appear to believe in this new (distorted) version of the character which he himself has created.

A natural comedian goes through these three stages almost simultaneously.

Let us take an extreme example of a role which lends itself to this treatment, Harpagon in Molière's great comedy *The Miser*. The actor playing this part will have no difficulty, after seeing the character as a whole, in selecting greed as the dominant trait in the man. Having done this he must appear to believe in this character of an exaggeratedly avaricious man. Once this latter task has been successfully accomplished there will be less tendency to over-play the part, a common fault in comedy acting.

Another example from Molière is the hypocrite Tartuffe. From Shakespeare we have Falstaff, Bottom, Dogberry, Parolles and a host of others, each a little larger than life.

Most beginners find it difficult to adopt the comic attitude and prefer to perform in serious plays where they can give 'sincere' performances—usually over-emoted and over-tense. The objective approach to a character often comes, if it comes at all, with maturity and experience. Moreover, the glitter and sparkle associated with most types of comedy are out of the range of the slow mover and thinker. Nevertheless, the external tricks are not too difficult to teach and once some of these have been mastered and the laughter of an audience heard as a result, the student begins to like the medium. A mechanical approach often helps him to acquire the essentials. Thus I have made slower pupils accelerate their rate of speech and movement before they rehearsed a comic scene, and their performances then often gained in liveliness and sparkle. When employing this method I have warned the student that at first the quicker tempo would seem very artificial to him but if he persevered this feeling would disappear.

Comedy Business

When the beginner has succeeded in acquiring the Comic attitude to life and the ability to see characters in perspective, he must attempt to master some of the tricks of comic acting which are so effective in raising laughter. Such are the double-take, the pointing and throwing away of lines, the use of repetition and contrast.

Double-take (or *double-takem*). This is a favourite trick of comedians. It means that the presence of something or somebody has registered in your brain twice—one after the other. The second image is sharper than the first and gives rise to the comic reaction. Here is a simple example—

Imagine that you are in a good mood as you enter your office, humming a gay tune, and cheerfully singing out, "Good day" to your visitor whom you pass to put your hat on the rack. You stop suddenly when you realise that this visitor is a man with a knife who is waiting to attack you. Your change of expression and mood when 'the penny drops' will give the comic effect which causes laughter. The first image of the intruder was blurred, probably because you were in too good a mood to expect such a visitor; the second image was more sharply defined and made you take appropriate action.

The *frozen smile* is a variation of this effect. Suppose that somebody is maligning a few of your acquaintances in a caustic but rather witty manner. You laugh loudly as he names their weaknesses. But your laughter changes to a frozen smile followed by a fixed expression of tight-lipped anger when you realise that the last person he was referring to was yourself.

Both these tricks rely on their effectiveness on your appearing to do things mechanically and then being brought back to full awareness of the situation with a sharp jolt.

Pointing and Throwing Away Lines

By putting a pause before a word, line or phrase it can be made to stand out in relief. This is very useful in comedy as may be seen in Experiment 10, for it helps to prolong the comic tension which finds its safety valve in laughter.

Apart from actually speaking the laugh line in a louder voice and with a more incisive manner, there is another device which can be used to good effect. This is to 'throw away' the line, i.e. speak it in a *softer* voice than the lines which have preceded it. For instance, in the sentences

"Augustus is a very brave man. At least so they tell me." If the first sentence is given due emphasis and the second one under-stressed or 'thrown away', the latter will probably be greeted with laughter, the implication being that you do not share other peoples' opinion of Augustus. The knack of throwing away lines effectively is difficult to acquire for some actors. It is all too easy to deliver the line or phrase too softly so that the audience does not get the point of the whole sequence.

Repetition

The music hall comedian who repeats the same catch phrase on different and often inappropriate occasions is using another well tried piece of comedy business. Such phrases as 'Can I do you now, Sir?' and, 'It's all in the mind you know' evoke a chuckle whenever they are heard. These lines are not funny in themselves but repetition on the radio has made them so to habitual listeners.

Pieces of Stage Business can be made to appear funny if repeated, as though mechanically. When this mechanical repetition is interrupted, laughter greets the performance. The man who bites his thumb in agitation on two or three separate occasions and stops just as he is about to do it again will get his laugh if his comic timing is good enough.

Charged Dialogue in Comedy.

Comic Dialogue often contains lines charged with a concealed meaning. In Noel Coward's *Private Lives* Ellyot is ostensibly telling Amanda that the Taj Mahal was 'Unbelievable, a sort of dream' when in actual fact he is referring to her (Amanda's) appearance.

The Comedy of Manners.

This is a specialised type of High Comedy and a great deal of skill and experience is required of the actor who wishes to master it. He must first steep himself in the modes and manners of the period concerned and acquire a fine awareness of the style. In the playing there should be a lack of violent emotion even in the face of circumstances which normally require it. This aloofness is exemplified by Lady Bracknell's calm treatment of the matter of the loss of a baby almost as though it were the mislaying of a favourite book. The wooing of Millamant by Mirabell is another example of serious things not taken too seriously.

Wycherley, Congreve, Sheridan and Wilde each in his own way wrote this type of High Comedy and students can gain much by reading their plays, or better still, by seeing them performed well. The acting requires an elegance in dress, precision in movement and gesture and a sharpness of delivery of the lines. It also requires a knowledge of the cadences of English Prose and a true feeling for them.

Farce

In this type of comedy incongruous and unreal things take place against a naturalistic background. Thus in *Thark*, by Ben Travers, the setting is one of the stately homes of England. Here people chase ghosts with guns; trapdoors and sliding panels abound, and there is a butler called Death, who hisses rather than speaks. The actor playing in farce must keep a straight face even in the most ludicrous situations. The more serious he remains the funnier he will be. There is a tendency to giggle when acting in this type of play; it must be restrained, otherwise the comic illusion will be broken.

When Laughter is Out of Place.

There are many actors, well versed in comedy technique, who try to obtain laughter by unfair methods. They will reverse the order of words, introduce irrelevant funny business, and even change the obvious meaning of a line in order to obtain a cheap laugh. Such are not to be imitated. They destroy the balance between what is subtle and what is crude. In farce certain excesses of this nature are allowed. Custard Pie Comedy and slapstick methods, however, are out of place in the general run of the more subtle plays in the Comic Spirit.

Experiment 10 deals with a typical comic sequence which builds up to a laugh line. It is taken from Act II of Pinero's *Preserving Mr. Panmure*.

EXPERIMENT 10. AIM: TO DISCOVER COMEDIC RHYTHM

Number involved: 3 women.
Characters:

 Mrs. Lottie Panmure — wife of the owner of "Clewers" the country house where the scene is set.

Miss Dulcie Antice   — her sister.
Mrs. Hebblethwaite   — her aunt.
Period 1910.

The Situation.

The women have learned that one of the men in the house has kissed the attractive young governess. Each woman in turn suspects her husband or fiancé.

Stage 1. The following text, *but with the stage directions omitted,* is given to the students for study.

Mrs. Hebblethwaite.	(Putting her hand to her bosom) Oh, Lottie, Oh, Dulcie (sinking into the armchair by the fauteuil stool D.R.) Oh, my dears.
Dulcie.	(Under her breath) Oh-h (To Mrs. Panmure in a whisper) Crikey.
Mrs. Panmure.	(To Dulcie) No, no.
	(Dulcie shrugs her shoulders. Mrs. Panmure hurries to Mrs. Hebblethwaite).
	Oh, no, Auntie!
Dulcie.	(Also going to Mrs. Hebblethwaite) Impossible.
Mrs. Hebblethwaite.	(Tearfully) My dears, this would not be the first time your uncle has stabbed me to the heart.
Dulcie.	(Sitting on fauteuil stool) No!
Mrs. Hebblethwaite.	Years ago—at Harrogate—a creature in the hotel—a hussy with a ridiculous waist . . .
Mrs. Panmure.	(Taking Mrs. Hebblethwaite's hand) Ah!
Mrs. Hebblethwaite.	I walked on to the tennis court one morning and confronted them.
Dulcie.	(with zest) What happened?
Mrs. Hebblethwaite.	(struggling to her feet) I was fined a shilling for damaging the turf with my heels. (She walks U.L. in great agitation).

Stage 2.

Directions Given.

Play the above scene seriously, imagining that Mrs. Hebble-thwaite's certainty that her husband is the culprit will have tragic consequences. At the beginning of the scene your positions are as follows—

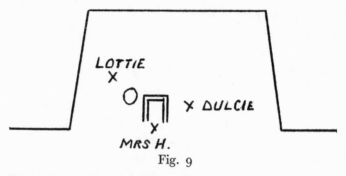

Fig. 9

To Mrs. Hebblethwaite. Do not give the words too much attack particularly the obviously comic lines. As far as you are concerned this is the end of your marriage.

There will be very little movement in the scene. Mrs. H. is sitting in the armchair D.R. with Dulcie to the Right and Lottie to the Left of her.

Stage 3.

The students are shown the full text, containing the stage directions as given above. The scene is to be played again, bringing out the full flavour of the comedy.

Directions Given.

At the beginning of the scene your positions are as shown in Fig. 10.

To Mrs. Hebblethwaite. Give the sequence its full weight and attack. Dramatise the situation so that the performance is if anything larger than if it were in a really tragic play. The tempo is

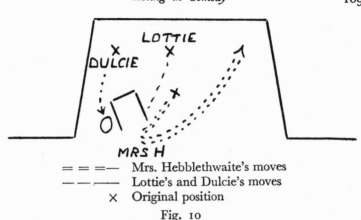

= = =— Mrs. Hebblethwaite's moves
— — .—— Lottie's and Dulcie's moves
× Original position

Fig. 10

quicker than before. The last line is the one that should receive
the loudest laugh so point it with a pause as you struggle to your
feet. It is important that this should be the clearest line of the
sequence. Consequently do not overpoint the line "My dears, this
is not the first time your uncle has stabbed me to the heart", as
this is not the climax.

To Dulcie and Lottie. You must both try and comfort Mrs.
Hebblethwaite even though Dulcie is quite ready to believe that
her uncle is a philanderer. Mrs. Panmure, cast in purer mould,
does not. Thus the little scene between these two is played upstage
and out of sight of Mrs. Hebblethwaite before they both hurry
to reassure her that uncle could not do such a deed. When the
aunt begins her story of the past misdeed, you must both show
great interest and keep up the comic tension by giving the
interjections "No", "Ah" and "What happened?" a sense of
urgency. This is further emphasised by Dulcie sitting on the
fauteuil stool, ready to hear more.

Notes.

1. The extract played in serious and then in comic vein was run

through several times until both scenes were performed to my satisfaction.

2. Other members of the class were present to observe the results of the experiment.

3. These performers were chosen from a more advanced class.

Comments.

The difference between the serious and comic performances can be summarised thus—

In the serious version (Stage 1)—

1. The tempo was slower.

2. The interplay between Lottie and Dulcie was given more emphasis. Thus Dulcie's first "Oh-h" was a cry of pain (the word 'crikey' was almost inaudible). Lottie's "No—no" was spoken as if she meant "this is terrible", with a pause between the two words.

3. Mrs. Hebblethwaite was quietly sobbing before they came to comfort her.

4. Dulcie instead of sitting on the fauteuil stool placed her hand gently on her aunt's shoulder.

5. Mrs. Panmure's interjection "ah" was full of portent.

6. Mrs. Hebblethwaite played down the comic content of her lines by controlling her tears as she spoke quietly, smiling bitterly at "A hussy with a ridiculous waist". "I walked on to the tennis court and confronted them" was delivered in a flat voice.

7. Dulcie asked "What happened?" gently.

8. The last line was delivered with a smile as if to say "All my suffering was just treated as a rather silly joke, that's all".

In the most effective comedy versions—

1. The tempo was quicker.

2. Reactions on the whole were quicker (Dulcie's 'No' as she sat on the stool was usually greeted with a titter on this account).

3. The interplay between Dulcie and Lottie was more conspiratorial, i.e. they tried to hide their reactions from their aunt.

4. Mrs. Hebblethwaite's sobs were louder until she controlled herself sufficiently to tell her story.

5. Mrs. Panmure's taking her aunt's hand and patting it covered the laugh which followed "a hussy with a ridiculous waist". This phrase was not unduly emphasised, thus ensuring that the climax of the scene was not spoilt.

6. Dulcie asked "What happened?" with great urgency.

7. Mrs. Hebblethwaite struggled to her feet without speaking, so that the half-expected anti-climax was well pointed.

8. The last line was given more attack than in the serious version.

9. The laughter which followed (the loudest in the sequence) was covered by the walk.

The sequence can be summarised thus—

i.   The approaching moves and dialogue which are preparatory to the major laugh lines. This includes the first four speeches (up to Dulcie's "Impossible").

ii. The stretching of the tension by the main dialogue and the interjections beginning with Mrs. Hebblethwaite's "My dears, this would not be first time . . ."

iii. The pause—or tension point after Dulcie's "What happened?".

iv. The release or laugh line.

v.   The relaxing move which covers the laugh.

Of course, not every performance exactly followed this pattern. It must be emphasised that this is only one type of laughter sequence; others can be discovered by experiment. There is a wide field for research in our native comedy. Other patterns are to be found in Congreve's *Way of the World*, Wilde's *The Importance of Being Earnest* and Coward's *Private Lives*. The Producer and Actor who can recognise the pattern will be immeasurably helped in his search for the often elusive laughter reaction of the audience.

Errors.

1. Speaking through the laughter of the audience. A common fault, which was partly obviated by the stage business, and, as already mentioned, by the use of relaxing moves. In the case of persistent offenders in this respect, they were asked to repeat certain lines and to follow with a pause which was filled in with a movement or gesture in keeping with the character and the situation. The laughter of the "audience" was often simulated to accustom the beginner to audience reaction.

2. Slow reaction which tended to drop the pace and so break the comic rhythm. This was corrected by running through the sequence several times until the performer got the feel of the scene. Watching the other students perform the two versions helped them to improve their own performaces with the minimum of directions from myself. In addition constant practice in quick reaction to the stage partner's dialogue was given in other exercises.

3. Slowness in taking up cues. Students noticed how this was deliberately done to good effect in the serious version but tended to spoil the comic rendering. This was eliminated by constant practice in dealing with quick fire dialogue as exemplified in some of Odets' plays. Other technical aspects were dealt with in the speech training classes. Faulty breath control is often the cause of tardy taking up of cues. For example, the beginner will take his breath after the last speaker has finished the line of dialogue; the result being that the scene is punctuated with false pauses.

4. Anticipation of cues, or cutting across other performers' lines. This occurred in both the comic and serious versions. It was usually due to over-anxiety to keep up the pace or to uncertainty of the cue line. This was usually put right by looking over the

script with the performers and pointing out where the lapses had occurred. The scene was then performed several times until the students were proficient in taking up their cues at the right time.

I would point out that deliberately overlapped dialogue is a comic effect often employed by playwrights and producers. This has its own special technique.

5. Hurrying through the scene in the mistaken idea that speed alone is the essence of comic acting. Although the over-all pace (or tempo) should be faster in the comedy version, there must still be that individual variation in pace, pitch, volume and emphasis which distinguishes all good acting. I have seen a performance of the muffin scene from *The Importance of Being Earnest* ruined by being rushed through at breakneck speed. The remedy lies in making the student slow down and unhurriedly perform each stage task as it occurs according to the above stage directions. The resultant tempo is at first slower than that required but the acting gains in variety in both voice and movement. If the scene is then played through two or three times it is found that the student adjusts himself to the correct tempo without losing the variety which is now enriching the performance.

Supplementary Exercises.

1. Comic Tension leading to a double-take.

Alice. George, I've always known that you were the kindest of men.

George. Did you really?

Alice. And the most chivalrous.

George. The most chivalrous!

Alice. I really mean that George—the kindest, the most chivalrous, the bravest . . .

George. The bravest! Oh, Alice!

Alice. So I thought . . .

George. (In a trance) Yes you thought . . .

8

Alice. I thought you were just the man to take the blame for what I did last night.

George. Take the blame . . . (realising what she means) TAKE THE BLAME. Good Lord.

The inane look on George's face as Alice bewitches him must change to one of alarm when he realises what she is up to. The mechanical repetition of 'take the blame' at first in an insipid manner and then loudly to register his horror, should obtain the desired laugh.

2. *The School for Scandal*—Sheridan, (*Act I, Scene* 1).

Mrs. Candour . . . Tale-bearers are as bad as the tale-makers—'tis an old observation, and a very true one: but what's to be done, as I said before? How will you prevent people from talking? To-day, Mrs. Clackit assured me, Mr. and Mrs. Honeymoon were at last become mere man and wife, like the rest of their acquaintance. She likewise hinted that a certain widow, in the next street, had got rid of her dropsy and recovered her shape in a most surprising manner. And at the same time Miss Tattle, who was by, affirmed that Lord Buffalo had discovered his lady at a house of no extraordinary fame; and that Sir Harry Bouquet and Tom Saunter were to measure swords on a similar provocation. But, Lord, do you think I would report these things! No, no! tale-bearers, as I said before, are just as bad as the tale-makers.

Crisp articulation and a buoyant manner is required to get the full value from this passage. It should be taken at a fast tempo so that the main laugh can be obtained on the last line, where Mrs. Candour's precept and practice so obviously differ.

3. *Much Ado About Nothing*—Shakespeare, (*Act IV, Scene* 1).

Beatrice and Benedick confess their love for each other.

Benedick. I do love nothing in the world so well as you: is not that strange?

Beatrice. As strange as the thing I know not. It were as possible for me to say I loved nothing so well as you; but believe me not, and yet I lie not; I confess nothing, nor I deny nothing. I am sorry for my cousin.

Benedick. By my sword, Beatrice, thou lovest me.

Beatrice. Do not swear by it, and eat it.

Benedick. I will swear by it that you love me; and I will make him eat it that says I love not you.

Beatrice. Will you not eat your word?

Benedick. With no sauce that can be devised to it. I protest I love thee.

Beatrice. Why then, God forgive me!

Benedick. What offence, sweet Beatrice?

Beatrice. You have stayed me in a happy hour. I was about to protest I loved you.

The comic tension is here built up to 'What offence, sweet Beatrice?' and then released by Beatrice's words, 'I was about to protest I loved you'.

This extract should provide the student with opportunities for delicate pointing and for the most subtle kind of Romantic Comedy Acting. It can be compared with the passage from *Still Life* which is used to illustrate the use of Charged Dialogue (page 80).

4. *A Hypochondriac*

From *The Proposal* by Anton Chekhov.

Lomov has come to propose to Natalya. He has been left alone for a moment by her delighted father who has rushed off to tell her the news.

Lomov. It's cold. I'm shivering all over, as though I were taking an examination . . . The main thing is to make up your mind. If you think about it for too long and talk and waver and wait for the ideal woman or for true love then you'll never get married . . . Brr—it *is* cold. Natalya Stepanovna is an excellent housekeeper, not bad looking, educated—what more do I want. But my head's beginning to hum with sheer excitement (drinks water). And I *must* get married. Firstly, I've reached thirty five—a dangerous age, you know. Secondly I need a regular well-ordered life. My heart's bad and it's continually palpitating. I'm so very excitable and I'm always in a nervous state. At this very moment my lips are quivering and my left eyelid is twitching. But my worst trouble is with sleep. I've hardly got into bed and started to doze off when something jabs me in my left side—jab. And it goes right through my shoulder up to my head. I jump up like a lunatic, walk about a little and then lie down again. But as soon as I begin to drop off—jab—there it goes again in my side. And it's the same thing twenty times over.

Remember that Lomov is really a healthy man. A robust appearance which belies the words he speaks will help to bring out the comedy, and the twitching of the eyelid and the quivering of the lips all add to it. His obvious excitement points to an agitated, nervous delivery of the lines.

SUMMARY

1. Audience laughter reaction can be planned by the actor and the producer. It often depends on tricks such as sharp contrasts, incongruities and repetition of stage business.
2. The comic actor when studying his role, must
   a. view the character from a distance,
   b. select one side of the character and distort it,
   c. believe in this new distorted version of the character.
3. Viewing the character from afar comes with maturity and experience.

4. Some of the Comedy tricks explained are the double take, the frozen smile, the pointing and throwing away of lines and phrases, repetition, contrast and the subtle employment of charged dialogue.

5. The Comedy of Manners is a specialised type of High Comedy. It requires from the actor an absence of emotion, elegance in dress and precision of speech, movement and gesture. The performer must also possess a feeling for the cadences of English prose.

6. *Farce.* In this type of Comedy unreal events take place against a naturalistic background. The actor must keep a straight face and believe in what he is doing.

7. Exaggerated and crude comic effects can destroy the balance of a play. Comedy tricks should be avoided when they are out of keeping with the style of the play.

8. When performing in a comic sequence the underlying pattern must be studied. Comic tension builds up to a laugh line.

9. The actor must not speak through the laughter of the audience. He must wait till it begins to subside.

10. Cues must be taken up promptly.

11. The tempo is generally faster than that of serious plays. In rehearsal, however, it is sometimes advisable to play certain sequences at a slower tempo so that essential points are not lost.

★ 12 ★

The Elements of Stage Movement

I t has already been said, when discussing the general requirements of the actor, that a relaxed body, free of muscular constriction is of vital necessity for his work. If he is too tense the channels
of communication to the audience will be blocked and the
performance will suffer. It is one of the chief aims of movement
training to make the body a relaxed instrument, ready to meet the
demands of the stage task. Just as the ballet dancer subjects
himself to a regular and often arduous system of limbering up,
so should the actor undertake to perform daily exercises which
help to keep him fit and to render his muscles supple and free of
excess tension. Here it must be stated that a certain amount of
tension and effort is required to successfully perform daily tasks
such as sitting, standing, walking and running. In fact every
action must be accompanied by the tensing of some muscle or
other; even standing upright without moving involves the action
of sets of antagonistic muscles. This last fact ought to be remembered by Drama students who walk about as though they
have no backbone. Slouching is not true relaxation for it merely
keeps important muscles in a state of permanent unemployment.

But Movement Training has a more positive aim. The body
must be helped to become more expressive and to delight in the
sheer joy of movement and physical activity. We often hear that
an artist has acted with his whole body; by this we mean that he
has acted in such a manner that all his physical resources have

been summoned to make his interpretation life-like and dramatic. The dying Richard the Third, as interpreted by Sir Laurence Olivier with his arms and legs thrashing the air, resembled a spider in its death throes. The actor's body was invested with the spirit of the character and expressed every nuance of Richard's thoughts and feelings. This standard of interpretation should be the aim of every student.

Lastly, our training should help to endow the student with a sense of rhythm which is so essential an element of good timing.

A Simple Routine.

Here are some simple exercises which should be performed daily as a limbering-up routine. The whole series need not take more than 15 minutes.

1. a. Stand with the feet apart and the arms hanging loosely by the sides. See Fig. 11(a)
   b. Bend forward with the head well down. The head and arms are relaxed, the knees are slightly bent. There should be no attempt to touch the floor otherwise stiffening of the body will result.
   c. Slowly stretch well up as though you were being pulled up to the ceiling by strings attached to your fingers.
   d. Relax into the bending position (as described in b) as though the strings attached to your fingers have been released.
   Repeat this eight times.

2. Slowly circle your head first to the left and then to the right— six times in each direction. Do this gently and stop immediately if you feel dizzy.

3. Rotate your left arm by your side (fig. 12) as though bowling overarm—Repeat six times.
   Do the same with the right arm.
   Repeat, rotating both arms at the same time.

Fig. 11
Exercise 1

Fig. 12

4. Balance on the right leg with hands on hips (fig. 13) and rotate the left leg five times.

Fig. 13

Balance on left leg and rotate the right leg five times.

5. Sit. Tense and relax your left foot by stretching and relaxing your toes—six times.

Repeat this with the right foot. Then shake each foot in turn until it feels loose.

6. Stand with the feet apart and the arms hanging loosely by the sides. Then bend forward slightly and rotate the trunk five times to the right—then five times to the left (fig. 14).

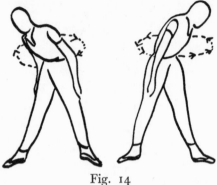

Fig. 14

7. Stand with the wrists in front of the body. Shake each wrist in turn until it feels loose and hangs as a dead weight. Then rotate the left wrist. Repeat with the right wrist.

8. Bend the body so that the upper trunk is parallel with the ground, with the arms stretched forward and the head upright. There should be a feeling of strain in the neck and the shoulders. Keeping the arms at shoulder level swivel them to the sides, then bring them back to the forward position (fig. 15). The head remains upright throughout. Swivel the arms

Fig. 15

forward and sideways six times, then relax into an upright position.

9. Finally, repeat Exercise 1.

At night the following exercise may be added to help you relax after the day's exertions:

10. Lie flat on the floor or on your bed, with a support such as a small cushion at the base of the neck. Let your body sink into the floor or into the bed until you feel it to be a dead weight. There will still be a point of strain somewhere—probably in the neck or in the shoulders. Now quite deliberately shift this point of tension to another part of the body, e.g. the spine, then to the legs, the feet and the toes. Then feel the point of tension reaching a shoulder and arm by way of your spine, eventually arriving at your hand which is lightly clenched. It may be either hand. Finally release the tension by opening the hand and allowing it to escape.

In this exercise the point of tension can be regarded as a small globule of mercury which travels quickly from one point of the body to another.

This simple routine taken in conjunction with the exercises on Contact with the Audience and the others dealing with Internal Technique will help to induce relaxation.

Good Posture.

The normal stance should be one of alert repose, neither too stiff nor too relaxed. Directions should be given as follows:

1. Feel taller than you are without actually rising on the toes.

2. Roll your shoulders, shrug them and let them sink into position, neither too far advanced nor too far back.

3. Feel a slight strain in the hollow of the back.

4. Choose a point at eye level about ten feet away and take four paces towards it.

The instructor must check that the body is not stiff, that the shoulders are not pulled back or advanced too far and that the head is not poked forward.

Stage Falls.

These can be considered as extensions of the relaxation exercises.

1. Stand upright in the good position as described above.
2. Gradually relax and sway backwards and forwards.
3. Sink on the knees and swivel as you touch the floor.
4. Roll from one side to the other as you land.
5. The head should reach the floor last.

This should be done slowly at first and gradually speeded up as confidence is gained.

Instinctive Movement.

We react instinctively if we are attacked. We do not reason but adopt an attitude of defence. Such instinctive reactions can be put to good use in Movement Training and the following experiment was tried to prove this.

EXPERIMENT 11.

No. of Characters: Nine.

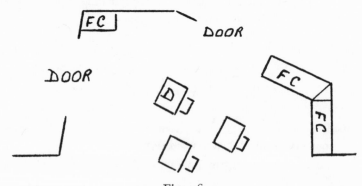

Fig. 16
Plan of furniture:
F.C. = Filing Cabinet   D. = Desk and Chair.

There is a quarrel taking place in the outer office of a large business organisation. All the employees in the main office get as near to the door R. as possible and crane their necks to hear what is being said. Suddenly the bell rings to summon one of the secretaries. This means that the director has returned and all the other employees resume their work at desks or filing cabinets in case he should come in and catch them idling. The instructor claps his hands to mark the beginning of the quarrel improvised by A. and B. A handbell is rung to summon the secretary. Act according to the situation without further directions.

Notes.

1. The quarrel in the outer office was improvised.

2. Each person was allocated a desk or filing cabinet with a definite task.

3. The sequence was repeated two or three times.

Comments.

1. Students further away from the door R. did not react to the sounds of the quarrel immediately. Apparently such was the atmosphere of fear in this office that some of the performers had pretexts ready for leaving their desks—they went to the filing cabinet U.R. with sheets of paper which were not intended to be filed. Others unashamedly went up to the door and craned their necks to hear every word.

2. When the bell sounded the secretary rushed to her desk to collect her notebook before making a quick exit.

3. Those who had pretexts for leaving their desks used more leisurely moves to return. One person remained at the filing cabinet U.R. and unabashedly continued to listen until the quarrel subsided.

4. The movement was spontaneous and natural. Very little would have to be done to weave it into the pattern of a production.

Common Errors.

1. When the exercise was repeated a certain amount of the spontaneity was lost by some of the performers anticipating the signals.

2. More subtle movements were introduced at the third attempt. Head turns were employed and people looked meaningly at each other. When this was overdone the sequence dragged and again the effect of spontaneity was lost.

Supplementary Exercise.

1. You are Prisoners of War planning an escape. Each person is given a job to do. As you are discussing this the guards unexpectedly arrive and you resort to subterfuge so as not to arouse their suspicions. Do this instinctively as you have no time to prepare excuses. Arrange the set so that there is plenty of opportunity for spontaneous movement.

Motivated Movement.

Normally we move on the stage with a definite motive and the author sometimes indicates this in his stage directions. Very often the motive has to be decided by the actor concerned (e.g. "I go to Joan to protect her" or "I cross to the mantelpiece to get myself a cigarette"). These motives are selected to fit in with the mood of the scene and with the general scheme of movement of the production. Indeed sometimes the moves are given arbitrarily by the producer and the actor has to find an inner justification for them. A thorough knowledge of the play will help him to do this and so give his performance that inner conviction which is the mark of the sincere artist.

Exercises in Motivated Movement.

1. Cross to the mantelpiece in order to
   a.   look at a photograph.
   b.   look for a match to light your cigarette.

c. warm your hands before the fire.

d. search for some money which you think you left there.

2. Cross to your stage partner in order to

a. protect him (or her).

b. scold him.

c. ask him something. (decide exactly what it is).

In both these exercises think of a definite situation in which your reason for moving is justified.

Unconscious Movement and Drifting Moves.

Not every move has a conscious motive. When deep in thought or worried we often move about seemingly without a definite purpose. This can be put to good use by the producer who wishes to re-arrange his grouping.

It must be remembered however, that such moves are the result of an inner compulsion. They are nature's safety valve for the release of tension. In our discussion of quarrel scenes (page 67) we have already seen how moves of this nature help in both the building up to a climax and in the subsequent release from tension.

Group Movement—Dressing the Stage.

Students should be given ample practice in dressing the stage, that is making artistic use of the space available when there are several people on the stage. This simple exercise will help.

Place as many students on the stage as possible, short of absolutely packing it. At a pre-arranged signal they are to start circulating without bumping into each other. On a second signal they are to stop moving and then space themselves out so that there are no huddled groups.

If this exercise is repeated several times students acquire confidence in making full use of the space available without being too self-conscious about it. It also helps the producer to arrange them in patterns and groups which enhance the pictorial side of the performance.

Moving in a Restricted Space.

Students often find it difficult to move about with ease and confidence in a limited acting area. The furniture and properties seem to get in the way. Constant practice in avoiding these obstacles is obviously necessary and exercises such as the following should be devised.

EXPERIMENT 12. AIM: TO LEARN TO MOVE IN A
RESTRICTED AREA.

One character.

Furniture required: Settee or armchair.

                      Small round table.

                      Chest or large trunk.

                      Bookcase.

                      Square table with three chairs.

A small area should be marked out on the stage.

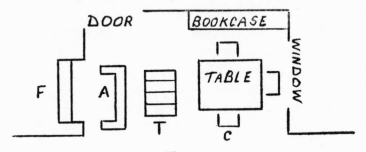

Fig. 17
Plan of furniture:
A = Settee.   T = Trunk.   C = Chair.   F = Fireplace.

The student is asked to move in this restricted area following a set route. The directions given are:

1. Enter by door U.R.
2. Go to the fireplace R. take down a vase from the mantelpiece.
3. Cross to the table L. and put down the vase.

4. Move above the table to the window.
5. Cross below table to the trunk, sidestepping the chair which is barring your way. Open the trunk, then close it again.
6. Cross to the bookcase U.L. and select a book.
7. Take the book to the settee R. and sink into it.

Stage 1.

Go through this series of movements mechanically. Avoid tripping over articles of furniture or bumping into them. Movements must be neat and precise. There should be no shuffling or looking around you.

This is repeated several times until the sequence is performed with confidence and precision.

Stage 2.

Repeat the exercise taking the same route, but this time find a reason for each move. For example ask yourself why you are going to the trunk, why you want the vase. Make up a situation into which all these movements will fit logically (e.g. looking for something).

Comments.

1. After two or three attempts the route was followed without hesitation, the student having automatically side-stepped, by-passed or even removed obstacles which lay in his path. This helped him with Stage Two when the movement was motivated and the exercise was no longer a mechanical one.
2. Definite types of turns were not prescribed. Too much attention can be paid to such niceties when the student can find out by practice the neatest way of changing direction.

Battle Scenes.

Scenes of violence involving many performers need very careful planning by the producer. The actors must not lose control in the heat of the battle otherwise untidiness and injury may be the result. Each participant must be given a set routine of actions

9

and movement and at the same time must feel himself to be part of a team. This battle sequence will serve to illustrate these points:

Two opposing armies enter, led by their Commanders-in-Chief, and face each other, before the struggle begins.

1. Army A. enters first from U.L.
2. Army B. enters from D.R.
3. There is a pause as the leaders come forward to face each other (see fig. 18).
4. The Leader of A. gives his battle cry and clashes swords with his opposite number.
5. Each soldier finds his opponent, who has been chosen beforehand. They engage in a fight at close quarters. No actual weapons are used in the first rehearsals and the predetermined routine is carried out in mime. Each couple of opponents has a different series of actions. Here is a suggested routine for one couple. (X. and Y.). The weapons are swords.

   a. X. cuts at Y. with his heavy sword. Y. parries.
   b. They circle round each other.
   c. X. ducks as Y. slashes at his head.
   d. X. cuts at Y.'s right side. Y. parries.
   e. They separate, step back and try to cut at each others heads. They lock weapons and circle round.
   f. Y. trips and X. runs him through (under the left arm).

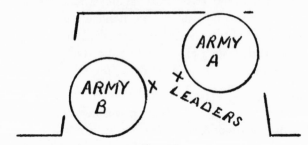

Fig. 18
The armies face each other

This routine is to be practised by the pair until it can be done without thinking. No deviation should be allowed otherwise accidents might occur. Y. should not slash at his opponents head until the latter has ducked!

6. The general battle will move in a clockwise direction, and the combatants, still fighting, will exit U.R. The Instructor will arrange the order of exit of each couple (see fig. 19).

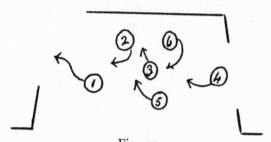

Fig. 19
The plan of exit:
← = direction of exit. Number indicates order of exit.

SUMMARY

1. The purpose of Movement Training is (a) to free the body of excess muscular strain and constriction and (b) to make the body more expressive.

2. A simple daily routine consisting of 10 exercises is given. These will help to loosen the muscles. They should be supplemented by exercises in mime, dancing, fencing, etc.

3. Good posture helps the performer to adopt a state of alert repose.

4. Stage falls should be practised as an extension of relaxation exercises.

5. Three types of movement are used on the stage.
    a. motivated movement—movement for a purpose.
    b. instinctive moves (e.g. to resist attack).

     c.   unconscious moves—these denote an inner state (e.g. walking up and down when restless).

6.   Students must learn to 'dress' the stage, i.e. make the best use of the space available. This helps the producer to arrange his grouping. Practice must also be obtained in moving in a restricted space without awkwardness.

7.   Battle scenes must be carefully planned by the producer, and the actors must adhere to the routine laid down by him. Good team work is essential if such scenes are to be effective.

★ 13 ★

Voice and Speech for the Stage

ON the stage the audible, well modulated voice is absolutely essential. Without it a good play will appear to be dull and undramatic and the defaulter will irritate rather than entertain the unhappy listener.

It is necessary to distinguish between the terms *Voice* and *Speech*.

VOICE is instinctive; we are endowed with it at birth. A child makes some sort of crying or cooing sound (i.e. gives voice) long before it has learnt, by trial and error, repetition and correction, the complex series of sounds which constitute speech. In adults we can recognise the general quality of the voice by describing it as pleasant, deep, shrill, harsh or strident. We can often recognise a person's voice before we can hear what he is actually saying, for no two persons' voices are absolutely identical.

SPEECH, on the other hand, is an acquired habit and depends on many factors, including the environment and education of the speaker. Two people can have the same accent because they live in the same town. Their manner of pronouncing vowels is the same. In such a case their modes of *speech* are said to be identical.

In brief, *Voice* is a general quality by which one person can be distinguished from another, while *Speech* is that more precise quality which deals with human utterance and communication of thought.

AIMS OF SPEECH TRAINING

It is the dual purpose of Speech Training to perfect the use of the *voice* so that it is pleasant and audible, and at the same time to improve *speech* so that it is clear, well articulated and free from defects of utterance. If both these aims are achieved the actor will have at his command a well tuned instrument capable of meeting the heavy demands made upon it in the Theatre.

Here a warning must be sounded. A well-tuned instrument alone is not enough. The performer must be endowed with imagination and sensitivity otherwise the instrument will not give of its best. For this reason speech training should not be divorced from the other work. It should operate side by side with exercises which enrich the student's experience and so make him capable of communicating to the audience the thoughts and emotions of a human being instead of the mouthings of a puppet.

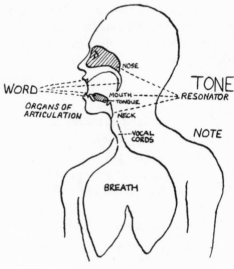

THE VOCAL APPARATUS

Fig. 20

THE HUMAN VOCAL INSTRUMENT

The theory of voice production can be appreciated by studying the diagram. (Fig. 20).

In human speech the following takes place:

1. The outgoing *breath* from the lungs forms a column of air in the windpipe.
2. This column of air presses against the vocal cords (which are akin to two elastic bands close together and stretched across the throat) and forces them to open and shut rhythmically thereby making a sound. This is called the *note*.
3. This sound is re-inforced as it passes through the neck, mouth and nose which together constitute the human resonator. These are said to have imparted *tone* to the note.
4. The organs of articulation (the lips, tongue, teeth, hard and soft palate) come into play to frame the *word* which is the unit of human speech.

The process can thus be divided into four aspects, these being Breath, Note, Tone, Word. All systems of Speech Training take them into account.

Although it is beyond the scope of this volume to deal with any particular system of Speech training in detail, a simple daily routine of exercises is once again recommended. A qualified instructor should be in attendance until they are mastered, after which they should form part of the student's daily 'five finger exercises', together with the movement routine (see page 119). They are arranged according to the aspects of voice production already mentioned. Once again relaxation exercises come first, for the body must be free of tension before the full benefit of the routine can be felt.

RELAXATION

1. Stretch upwards then release the tension by relaxing

into the bending position, as described in the movement routine (page 119).

2. Shake the hands and arms until they feel loose and relaxed.

3. Rotate the head to the left and then to the right—six times in each direction.

BREATHING

Increasing the Supply.

4. Adopt the relaxed upright stance you have already practised in your movement exercises. Place the knuckles of your hands so that they can feel the sides of the lower ribs. Breathe in gently to a count of two-three, meanwhile

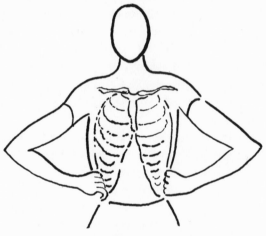

Fig. 21

feeling the expansion of the chest wall with your knuckles. Breathe out to the count of two-three. Do not raise the shoulders and keep the abdomen firm without it being tense. Maximum expansion should be in the region of the lower chest at the level of the sixth and seventh ribs.

Repeat this exercise twelve times to the rhythmic beat of IN-two-three—OUT-two-three. Do not force the pace. The ribs will swing upwards and outwards and will gradually increase the supply of breath that you are able to take.

Gaining Control.

5. Breathe in to the count of IN-two-three. Control the outgoing breath by counting the numbers one to ten aloud. Increase this at the rate of five numbers a week until you can count thirty without strain.

6. Breathe in deeply to the count of IN-two-three. Hold your breath to the count of HOLD-two-three. Keep the chest expanded by holding the ribs in their extended position, and expel the breath only from the base of the lungs by contracting the abdominal muscles to a count of PRESS-two-three. Slowly let the ribs descend.

TONE

N.B. We do not deal with the *note* at this stage as the muscles of the vocal cords cannot be consciously controlled by us. In any case the vocal note is never heard without the influence that the resonators have had on it. If they are functioning well, the final result must be satisfactory.

7. Let the jaw drop until the teeth are an inch apart. Close it again. Repeat this ten times.

   The open jaw is necessary to give the vowels their richest quality. The tongue tip should rest against the inside surface of the lower teeth. The lips should not be drawn back at the corners.

The next exercise should not be done until the resonator scale of vowels has been mastered. There are thirteen simple vowels in spoken English. They can be remembered by the sentence WHO WOULD KNOW AUGHT OF ART MUST WORK AND THEN TAKE HIS EASE. Their manner of formation is shown in the diagram.

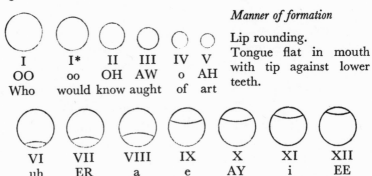

Lip rounding.
Tongue flat in mouth with tip against lower teeth.

Manner of formation : Body of tongue rising towards roof of mouth. Tongue tip against lower teeth.

Fig. 22 *Resonator Scale*

The following points are to be borne in mind when studying the chart.

1. Vowels I to V are formed by rounding the lips from the smallest opening at OO to the largest at AH. The tongue tip rests against the surface of the lower teeth. The body of the tongue is relaxed and the jaw is open so that the teeth are an inch apart. The circles represent the degree of opening formed by the rounded lips.

2. Vowels VI to XII are formed by the jaw remaining open. The tongue tip rests against the inner surface of the lower teeth with the body of the tongue progessively rising from a flat position and reaching its highest point at EE. The arc within the circle represents the position of the body of the tongue.

3. The vowels in large print are the main (long) vowels. Those in small print are subordinate (short) vowels.

4. Although OH and AY are treated as simple vowels, they are really diphthongs (see below).

Now that some knowledge of the formation of the vowels has been gained, the student can continue with the exercises on Tone.

Exercise 7.

a. Hum Mm on a convenient note (about the centre of your range). The tone should be supported by a sufficiency of controlled breath, and should be 'placed' forward on the lips. This can be checked by plucking the lips with your finger when they will emit a quivering sound.

b. From the humming transfer the tone to the vowel AH. Starting with a convenient note sing Mm—AH—Mm up and down the scale.

c. Repeat the exercise, this time transferring the tone to OO, thus: Mm—OO—Mm.

d. Intone a sentence containing the vowel OO on a convenient note around the middle of your range. The sentence can easily be made up by yourself. An example is: A gloomy view of the blue sea is taken by Saucy Sue. Repeat this six times. Immediately following the intoning speak the sentence so that the same quality is preserved. There should be no pause between the intoning and the speaking of the sentence.

e. Repeat the exercise with the other vowels. Four vowels each day should be chosen for practice.

Apart from the thirteen simple vowels of the resonator scale there are several compound vowels. An example is the sound in BUY which consists of the two vowels *uh* (VI) and *i* (XI). The emphasis is laid on one vowel and there is a glide to or from it. In the example chosen the stress is on the *uh* and there is a glide towards *i*.

The main *diphthongs*, consisting of two vowels are

I	uh-i	buy
OW	uh-oo	how
OI	AW-i	boy
U	i-OO	new

There is also a group consisting of simple vowels followed by a short *er*

OOR	oo-er	poor
ORE	AW-er	more
AIR	e-er	fair
EAR	i-er	dear

Yet a third group consists of triple vowel sounds (triphthongs) They are formed by the addition of *er* to some of the diphthongs.

OUR	uh-oo-er	shower
IRE	uh-i-er	fire
URE	i-oo-er	sure

Exercise 8.

Practise dividing the compound vowel into its simple vowels. Then sound each vowel 4 times separately thus:

huh huh huh huh hoo hoo hoo hoo

(the *h* is prefixed so as to prevent too sharp an initial attack on the vowel).

Finally join the two together by gliding from the *huh* to the *oo* huh-oo huh-oo huh-oo.

Repeat this with other compound vowels.

THE WORD

The vowels are associated with the general tone of the voice. They are the result of the unbroken passage of the note through the resonator. Consonants, however, are formed when this passage is blocked by the partial or complete closure of the resonator; in this way they give a definite shape to vocal sound and are associated with speech, or more precisely, with the *word*.

Consonants are classified by voice experts in several ways. For our purpose this simplified form of grouping is employed:

VOICED	VOICELESS EQUIVALENT
(the vocal cords vibrate)	(the vocal cords do not vibrate)
D	T
B	P
G (GOOD)	K
TH (THIS)	TH (THICK)
V	F
Z	S
ZH (PLEASURE)	SH
J (JUMP)	CH (CHURCH)
M	—
N	—
NG	—
L	—
R	—
—	H

Before the consonants are tackled the organs of articulation should be toned up with these simple exercises:

Exercise 9.

Open the jaw; extend the tongue until it comes to a point, then retract it—Repeat six times.

Exercise 10.

Open the jaw and move the tongue tip up and down so that it alternates in position between the back of the top teeth and the back of the lower teeth. No sound should be made.

Exercise 11.

Push the lips forward then relax them—repeat six times.

Exercise 12.

Curl your upper lip and try to touch your nose with it.

Exercise 13.

Curl your lower lip and try to touch your chin with it.

We can now continue with practice in the formation of consonants.

Exercise 14.

Practise the articulation of D B G T P K. They are called explosives because a light explosive sound accompanies their formation. This can be combined with vowel practice thus OOD DOO OHD DOH AWD DAW and so on through the Resonator Scale.

Exercise 15.

Repeat the exercise, this time with TH (voiced and voiceless) V F Z S.

Exercise 16.

Repeat MAH NAH NGAH several times, then substitute the other main vowels.

(Note: NG is formed by the back of the tongue rising to touch the soft palate which is lowered so that the air can pass through the nose).

These are called the nasal consonants.

Exercise 17.

Repeat LAH LAH LAH LAH to a definite rhythm several times. Vary this by substituting other vowels.

Exercise 18.

Practise the sounding of R at the beginning of words (REMAIN). The tongue tip is curled back.

R in an intermediate position (VERY). The tongue tip flaps once.

Trilled R (as it is pronounced in Scotland). The tongue tip flutters (thRRee, RRapid).

Now repeat *Very merry ready* six times without the trilled R, and six times with the trilled R.

Exercise 19.

Repeat OOS SOO OOZ ZOO OHS SOH OHZ ZOH and so on through the main vowels.

Exercise 20.

Repeat the above with SH and ZH thus OOSH SHOO OOZH ZHOO etc.

Exercise 14 to twenty should be supplemented by patter rhymes and tongue twisters such as those contained in Gwynneth Thurburn's *Voice and Speech*.

THE NOTE

We can now discuss the problems which concern the human note. Most of these are associated with the pitch and compass of the voice.

The compass of the singing voice is normally two octaves but the spoken voice does not employ the full range. In speech, when subtleties of inflection are to be indicated, the voice slides through fractions of tones and not through fixed notes as in singing. The prime necessity is not to have too high pitched or shrill a voice—this is unpleasant and is a symptom of over-excitement and neurosis. For the actor it spells lack of control.

In order to correct this fault it is first necessary to ascertain the centre note of the speaker's compass. Directions for effecting this are:

Sing LAH LAH LAH down the scale until you have reached the lowest comfortable note of which your voice is capable without rasping or croaking. Your centre note is an octave above this.

Hum the centre note and constantly use it in your exercises, particularly those on the vowels. In normal speech your voice should be pitched just below it.

In a long passage of an emotional nature the speaker should begin on a lower pitch so that he can build up to the higher one required by the climax. Intoning the first line of such a passage on or below the centre note several times, and then speaking it immediately afterwards will help to cure the student who tends to begin at too high a pitch. Speeches such as that of Marullus in Shakespeare's *Julius Caesar* (Act I) can be treated in this manner.

INTONATION

This is the rise and fall of the voice. It is determined by the emotional content of the spoken material, and by the meaning. Many exercises which are devised to help the student to acquire certain patterns of intonation result in his adopting mechanical inflexions. The chief offender is the producer who dictates every inflexion to his unfortunate victim. Intonation and inflexion, which are here treated as synonymous terms, are the outward expression of the personality, and imaginative exercises in Inner technique will help to enrich it and endow the actor with intonations which are meaningful and free of artifice.

This simple passage requires an intelligent approach to intonation if it is not to be rendered meaningless:

A. Here you, come here.

B. Do you mean me?

A. Yes, you.

B. Well, you'd better lower your voice when you speak to me.

A. Lower my voice? Why?

B. Because I'm not your servant, that's why.

A. What do you mean, not my servant?

B. What I say—Not your servant. Don't tell me that you speak like that to everybody.

A. I certainly do.

B. In that case you'd better do something about your voice. Good day!

FLEXIBILITY

A flexible voice is one which has the power of adjustment to any change of mood, emotion or thought. It is capable of ringing the changes and so keeping an audience alert and interested. A monotonous drone which marks the dead voice points to the need of energetic measures if its possessor wants to become an actor. First he should be given passages to tackle which will make him stretch his range (e.g. The Chorus from *Henry V* or Anne's speech in Act I, Scene I of *Richard III* beginning "Set down, set down Your honourable load") Exercises in singing up and down the scale should be performed. Counting 12345 to a rhythmic beat on an ascending and descending scale is another common exercise which can assist in curing the voice of remaining on one monotonous level.

VARIETY

Technically variety is obtained by changes in pace, pitch, volume and emphasis. The person who has something positive to say will use these aids without self-consciousness. If they are too consciously applied the resultant speech cannot but be artificial. The solution appears to be to give the student exciting work which will force him to use vital speech. Debates on subjects of topical interest and involving issues in which he is passionately committed to a definite point of view are of great value here. So is the study of major political speeches.

Finally Speech Training is an inexhaustible subject and only the broadest lines of procedure have been indicated here. A knowledge of Phonetics, Verse Speaking and Public Speaking should be part of the teacher's equipment. The background which these subjects provide will stand him in good stead as he assists the student with the practical work which is the latter's chief pre-occupation.

The following works are recommended for further study:
Voice and speech in the Theatre—J. Clifford Turner (Pitman).
Voice and speech—Gwynneth Thurburn (Nisbet).
Stage speech—L. Charteris Coffin (Herbert Jenkins).

SUMMARY

1. *Voice* is a general quality. It is instinctive and can be described as harsh, shrill, pleasant, etc.

2. *Speech* is a particular quality which is acquired. It refers to regional accent and articulation.

3. In the human vocal apparatus
   a. the air from the lungs provides the outgoing *Breath*, which
   b. presses against the vocal cords and forms the *Note*.
   c. This is re-inforced and given *Tone* in the human resonator which consists of the neck, throat and nose.
   d. The organs of articulation (lips, teeth tongue, hard and soft palate) impress their shape on the voice to form the *Word* which is the unit of speech.

4. Each of these four units—Breath, Note, Tone and Word must be made to function properly when training the human machine to meet the demands made upon it in the Theatre.

5. 20 exercises are given covering each one of these aspects. They should be learnt under the supervision of a qualified teacher, and then practised daily.

6. By *Intonation* is meant the rise and fall of the voice.

7. By *Flexibility* is meant adjustment of voice to change of mood without strain.

8. *Variety* of delivery is obtained by changes in pitch, pace, volume and emphasis.

9. The teacher is advised to study the subject in detail from the books which are recommended.

★ 14 ★

Characterisation: The Approach to the Role

WE have now arrived at the stage when it can be assumed that our actor is ready to undertake the ultimate aim of his work—the translation of the author's written text into live theatre. His role may be a small one consisting of a few lines or it may have the length and complexity of a Hamlet or a Lear—but the mode of coming to grips with it should be the same.

He should begin by reading the play—the *whole* play and not merely his own part. It is easy to forget that there are other characters besides your own—the actor is by the very nature of his work an egocentric person—but this first reading of the play is so important that it must not be omitted. If done along certain lines it will make that initial impact which is of greater value than all the analysing and theorising in the world.

THE FIRST READING

This is the advice given to the student-actor:—Read quickly, as though you were seeing and hearing the play in performance for the first time. This should be done even if you are thoroughly familiar with it. Do not pause or linger over any detail but press on until you come to the end of an act or scene. You must imagine that the same conditions are obtaining as those in a theatre with the audience around you. It may require a great deal of self-discipline but do not lay down the script until the final curtain has dropped. Now ask yourself these questions:

147

1.　Which part of the play gripped me most?
2.　With whom did I sympathise?
3.　Who were the chief characters?
4.　Which one of them made the strongest impact on me?
5.　How does my part fit in with the other characters—who are my friends and who are my enemies?
6.　Has the play any particular message. If so, what is it?
7.　What was the plot?

In this manner the actor is obliged to adopt a positive attitude towards the play. At the very least he has begun the preparatory work on his own role, but more important the rest of the play should provide him with abundant material to feed his imagination and to furnish him with pointers. At any rate he is now part of the whole—he is involved as a member of a team.

THE SECOND READING

The first impressions should be allowed to simmer for a while before the text is taken up again. Already the subconscious is at work selecting and rejecting certain aspects of the role—it should be allowed to continue undisturbed for a day or two, or even longer. Then and then only should the second reading be undertaken.

This time it is the student's own role which receives the bulk of his attention. As he reads he will begin to form more definite impressions of the character he is to portray. Only certain sequences will be re-read to confirm some of the first impressions and to reject others. Now and then he should halt and ask himself questions which have been prompted by the dialogue or the stage directions—"Why does he do this?" or "What is his reason for saying that?" Again, he will try to visualise the appearance—"Is he fat, thin, well built or puny looking?" and the temperament—"Is he excitable or phlegmatic?" After a time the lines will be read to conform with the picture of the character which is gradually shaping in the mind. Words spoken by other persons in the play will be noted if they refer to him, and oblique references to his personal habits in the stage directions will now have more relevance.

The purpose of the second reading, then, is to obtain a more definite idea of the character and to give it a firmer outline.

DIVISION OF THE ROLE INTO SECTIONS

Let us assume that our student has to come to grips with a major role—Hedda Gabler or Macbeth. The first two readings have been accomplished in the manner recommended and the questions have been answered on the play as a whole and on the character in particular. The task still seems insuperable—there is such a vast number of things to do, of obstacles to overcome. To make it easier the role should be divided into sections. Each section is really a sense unit and depends on what the character wants to do in that part of the play. Here is an example:

In Act I Sc. I of *King Lear*, the first entry of the aged monarch shows him to be in a generous mood—he is about to divide his kingdom among his three daughters, providing they express their dutiful love to him. Two of the daughters, Goneril and Regan, voice their affection in exaggerated and high flown language, and are duly rewarded. Cordelia, the third daughter. will not be a hypocrite. Although she loves her father she would rather say nothing than imitate her sisters' insincere flattery. Lear is furious and disowns her.

In this sequence the role of Lear divides itself into two obvious sections. The first begins when he is desirous of the flattery of his daughters, the second when he wants to punish Cordelia for her seemingly disloyal conduct. The transition between the two sections is marked by the pause which could follow Cordelia's "Nothing, my Lord" in reply to his

> "What can you say to draw
> A third more opulent than your sisters? Speak."

We can say that in the first section his objective was to reward his daughters while in the second it was to punish Cordelia.

The rest of the role can be similarly examined in order to find these divisions, each having an objective. These sections help the performer to find motives for his actions and to discover the meanings which underlie the written word. All this may add up to the answer to the most important question—"What is the character's main objective in the play as a whole?" often the answer is synonymous with the character's main ambition in life. In Macbeth it is, "To be king—to have power". In many a modern play the answer is, "To get to the top." In the study of many roles there are several conflicting motives and to select the main one which dominates the action is no easy problem; but the actor must solve the riddle otherwise he will not see his role in true perspective.

While engaged in this preparatory work the student should not remain static. He should not treat it as desk work or as a clinical analysis of a literary treatise. He should move about trying out inflections, mannerisms, gestures and stage business. All these will help him later in rehearsal providing they are not too fixed. The producer may have opposing ideas and it is as well to retain a pliable attitude in order to avoid the heartache which attends having to discard the too fondly nurtured bright idea or piece of business.

One warning must be given. It is this—"Do not wander too far afield so that the fringes of the play become more important than the body of it. One can too easily be led into sidepaths by attempting to discover how many children Lady Macbeth has when the answer is of very little practical use to the actress playing the part.

Our actor is now ready to attend the first rehearsal. He has something to give; he is familiar with the text and will not be at a complete loss when meeting the innumerable problems which are bound to arise. In short he should be a useful member of the cast, and a boon to any producer.

FIRST REHEARSALS

There are three types of producers:

1. The despot who will dictate every move and inflection.
2. The weakling who is at the mercy of his actors and will give in to their every whim.
3. The producer who will give directions, take suggestions and generally work in such a manner that his performers are inspired to do their best work.

In weekly repertory it is often the first of these types, the dictator, who holds the reins. There is little or no time available to indulge in such luxuries as trial and error and give and take. The play must be set by Friday, run through on Saturday morning and dress rehearsed some time on Monday before the first performance. Working to such a tight schedule may have its advantages—it prevents procrastination, a disease to which many artists are prone—but in the end the performance is machine-made. It has come off the conveyor belt, and very often without the finishing touches.

It is to be hoped that the inexperienced actor will not meet the second type of producer—the waverer. It is essential that somebody should be in charge of the production, and this type is hardly that. The stronger personalities of members of the cast will ride rough-shod over the plan of production, if plan there is, to the detriment of the performance.

We hope that our newcomer will meet the third type—the genuine artist who moulds the members of the cast into a team. He is patient yet firm, he knows when to force the pace and when to slow down, he can cajole and reprimand and yet his actor does not take offence. Such a person often speaks in a whisper but he commands more attention than the strictest of army disciplinarians.

Usually in early rehearsals the setting of the actors' moves has the first consideration. Whatever the type of producer that has fallen to our novice's lot he must try to adapt himself to his methods. He will accept dictated moves and make them his own by supplying motives. He will try to fit them in with the tempo of the production. All that he has learnt in movement classes will come to his aid. For now he will be reaping the full benefit of his training.

With the best type of producer a discussion of the play and the characters will precede the setting of the moves. Unfortunately this is the exception rather than the rule. If it does take place our student will take full advantage of this opportunity to compare other people's opinions with those he has acquired himself in the preparatory work on the role.

Ideally, early rehearsals should be conducted in a spirit of trial and error with the producer in charge. Moves are given, the actor tries them out, he appears uncomfortable, another is suggested and eventually the action clicks. In actual practice however the setting period is usually rushed through at breakneck speed.

THE MIDDLE PERIOD

Having learned the moves and made them part of his performance the next stage is to begin to learn the lines. If a definite time limit is not set for this he should try to learn them as he goes along in rehearsal so as to fit in with the moves. In any case the pernicious habit of learning by rote should be avoided. In our exercises in the handling of properties and in good timing he has had practice in co-ordinating speech with gesture and movement and this will stand him in good stead now. Away from rehearsal he will move about as he learns and not sit still unless it is called for in the text. If he is faced with a quarrel scene, with the help of the producer he will try to discover its underlying rhythm and meaning, will rehearse with his stage partner so that the sequence mounts to its climax and subsides. If he is given the formidable job of acting as Prologue he will use the knowledge he has gained in the experiments in contacting the audience. The result of a thorough training will now bear fruit.

LATER REHEARSALS

There is always a stage in rehearsal when no progress seems to be made—the doldrum period which every actor and producer must recognise. The lines have not yet become part of the actor and it is the prompter who seems to be doing most of the work. It is really a period of struggle, of impatience with oneself and with others—for what had been smooth with the book in one's hand has now become disjointed and unco-ordinated. Fortunately this phase soon passes and the play moves forward once more.

By now the performer should be cloaking himself in his role. This is sometimes a fast, sometimes a slow process, depending on the individual. The make-up is usually thought of at this stage. Charts are often used to help the novice if the character is a grotesque or somebody out of the ordinary. He will have been fitted for the clothes he will require for the performance and if possible will wear them in rehearsal. The real properties will come to hand and he must make further adjustments for so far he has been imagining or miming the stage business or using substitute properties, the latter being the more satisfactory procedure.

Meanwhile rehearsals become a matter of urgency and the finishing touches are being put in by the producer. Alterations in tempo (the over-all speed of a sequence) and in individual pace are effected. Certain movements are altered to fit in with groupings. Strangely enough the good actor does not feel like a puppet at this stage—he usually knows that the alterations are necessary and co-operates to the full in carrying them out. Mercifully there are, or should be, many rehearsals when sequences or whole scenes are run through without their being stopped by the director, who acts as a valuable sounding board. This helps the performer to gain confidence, to acquire continuity. Soon the next landmark looms near—the Dress Rehearsal.

DRESS REHEARSALS

There is a popular superstition that a bad Dress Rehearsal will ensure the success of the first night of the show. This is wishful thinking. A calamitous Dress Rehearsal is bound to be followed by improvements in the subsequent performance but by then it is usually too late for the first night to reach concert pitch. There should be three Dress Rehearsals. The first is not really a Dress Rehearsal at all. It is really a co-ordination rehearsal when the set, lighting, effects and actors come together for the first time. This is a frightening experience for the uninitiated. Doors will unexpectedly appear and open inwards instead of outwards, music will blare forth in the wrong places and spotlights will fade in and out at the climaxes of the most passionate scenes of love or hate. For the last time the actor must be prepared to be a puppet and to be moved about and have his positions altered to fit in with the other elements of the production. Interruptions will inevitably occur but he must not be unduly disturbed by them. His performance is bound to suffer but allowances should be made for this—not least by the actor himself. In the next Dress Rehearsal he ought to come into his own again. Perhaps the harassed producer will take more notice of him instead of the mere mechanics.

In the second Dress Rehearsal there will be fewer interruptions—the lessons learned from previous errors will have resulted in a smoother show. Mishaps will probably still occur but he will take them in his stride—perhaps his performance is becoming shockproof.

At the final Dress Rehearsal there should be an audience

present and mercifully there will be no interruptions. Now for the first time he will have the foretaste of the first night of the run of the show. He may want to make adjustments to his performance, but theatrical etiquette dictates that this must not be done without prior agreement with the producer and with his stage partner. He is now ready to face his ordeal.

THE PERFORMANCE

First night nerves are the price one has to pay for being an actor. The greatest artists suffer from this malady. So much hangs in the balance on this one night after weeks of rehearsal, that the dread of failure is the natural outcome. These taut nerves can be put to good use. They can induce that feeling of alert expectancy which is useful in meeting the challenge of the audience—they can serve as a springboard in launching off the performance. Once the first entrance is made the 'nerves' usually disappear as though by magic. Those who really suffer torments from this occupational disease should perform the relaxation exercises described on page 135 about a quarter of an hour before the first entrance. Deep breathing exercises are often a great help in giving additional relief. It is also advisable to be at the theatre as early as possible so as to reduce last minute bustle and worry to an absolute minimum.

The relief which follows the completion of the first performance must not lull our student into a feeling of security even if the newspaper criticisms have been flattering. Each night he must attempt to repeat what he has learnt in rehearsal and to charge himself with purpose in spite of an often unwilling spirit. This is no easy matter.

Thus the summit of the teacher's endeavours has been reached. The novice has endured his baptism of fire and it is hoped that he has not been scarred in the process. It is then that the teacher ought to begin to feel that his work has been worth while.

SUMMARY

1. The script should be read several times. Each reading should have a definite purpose.

2. The first Reading. The actor should read the whole play as though he were seeing it for the first time. He should then ask himself several questions in order to adopt a positive attitude to the play.

3. The second reading should be undertaken when an interval has elapsed since the first reading. He can now stop to examine the character more closely.

4. The role should be divided into sections to facilitate study. He must determine the main purpose of the character in the play.

5. The student should not remain static while studying the part but integrate the lines with movement and stage business.

6. The actor must adapt himself to the type of producer and the latter's methods.

7. In early rehearsals there is generally a discussion of the play after which the moves are set.

8. In later rehearsals the moves are consolidated, the role develops, the make-up is studied, alterations in tempo are tried out, sequences are run through without a stop.

9. Dress Rehearsals. Ideally there should be three.
   The *first* should be a co-ordination rehearsal for welding the set, lighting and effects together. It is often interrupted by the producer.
   The *second* is employed as a run through of the play in full costume with the errors in the first dress rehearsal no longer present.
   The *third* is a full scale Dress Rehearsal before an invited audience.

10. The Performance. First night nerves are inevitable. They should be used to charge the performance with purpose. Subsequent performances must not be allowed to sink to the level of a mechanical routine.

★ 15 ★

Conclusions

IT only remains to take a bird's eye view of the experiments and exercises which have been described, and to determine the part they will play in a general course of instruction in the technique of acting.

It will be seen that the system of training adopted has owed much to many of the schools of acting described in the first chapter. The attempt has been made to incorporate what was felt to be the best of each into a general scheme of work. Hence the experiment on Emotion Memory owes a great deal to Stanislavsky while the exercises in Comedy acting owe much to the Representational school. Many experiments did not result in proof of their deserving adoption in the course and these have not been described in this book.

Why experiment at all? The answer is simple. An experimental approach does not copy slavishly, it does not accept the new for the sake of novelty and it takes very little for granted. And so, by noting progress and observing common errors, the experimental worker can accept what is suitable for his purpose and reject what is unsatisfactory.

A three year course in the technique of acting is set out in Appendix I. It consists of:

1. A general syllabus of the subjects to be covered; the order in which these are listed is recommended as the one to be employed in the first four terms. Later the individual needs of the pupils ought to determine when specific exercises are

employed again. In actual practice the instructor will find that variations of the original exercises should be of use throughout the course.

2. A syllabus in which recommended activities are listed on a terminal basis. At the end of the third term an acting test should be given to each student. This can be quite an event and the climax of much individual preparation. It also helps the instructor to take stock of the student's progress after a year's work. The solo passages chosen should not be treated as pieces for recitation, but rather as examples of contact with the audience. Similarly the sequence chosen for the duologue should serve as an example of acting with the stage partner, as treated in Chapter IV. A more advanced test should be set at the end of the sixth term. In this case teams should be chosen for the group work and some kind of competition devised with a prize for the best team. In these tests a three point scale of marking is recommended (e.g. A B C for good, fair, and poor performances respectively).

Throughout the course the timetable will include Speech Training and Movement Practice. Mime, dancing and fencing must also form part of the curriculum. In this way the Internal and External equipment of the actor will be trained side by side.

It is hoped that the teacher will devise his own experiments and exercises to add to those given. In anticipation of this being the case the following remarks are intended to be of guidance:

1. Where the student's imagination is actively engaged there is a greater chance of the experiment being a success. Improvisation is of great help here. It does not follow however that a mechanical approach should be ruled out. The experiment on timing (page 89) is a case in point.

2. At all stages of training there must be constant review of the progress that both groups and individual students have made in all branches of technique so as to ensure that no one element is introduced prematurely or too late. The concept of timing, for instance, if introduced too soon, can result in an inhibited type

of performer who is afraid that his every move is being mis-timed. It is sometimes difficult to determine the right moment to introduce a new subject and to know when the student is ready for it.

3. Before introducing more advanced exercises in Internal Technique one must be certain that the pupil has reached the same stage in his vocal and movement training. For instance Shakespearian speeches should not be attempted until the student is proficient in breath control, resonance and in the general modulation of the voice, otherwise discouragement might result.

4. At all stages of his development the embryo artist must be given the feeling of confidence that he can perform the tasks he has been set. For this reason begin with the simplest exercise and gradually introduce more difficult ones.

5. There usually comes a stage when the student feels so confident of his ability that he thinks he can dispense with technique. He should be allowed to enjoy this new found freedom for a while before the more difficult part of the training is undertaken. This interim period is needed for consolidation of what has been learnt.

6. Even the most proficient actor can easily be cast down and his performance spoilt by untoward criticism. Destructive criticism serves no purpose. Faulty playing needs tactful correction in most cases. During the course the pupil's attitude varies between that of passionate self-criticism alternating with periods of exaggerated self-confidence. A certain amount of indulgence on the part of the instructor is necessary, for a mercurial temperament is natural to one whose work often entails emotional strain. This must not be allowed to lapse into an undisciplined attitude towards the work in hand, for the Theatre is the most exacting of masters.

Finally, the teacher will find that the training of the actor is no easy task. There are many obstacles in the path. If I have helped to remove some of them I shall feel more than amply **rewarded.**

APPENDIX I

Three Year Course in Acting Technique

A. GENERAL SYLLABUS OF SUBJECTS TO BE COVERED

1. General requirements of the actor.
2. Release of muscular tension.
3. Solo contact with the audience. Prologue and narrative work.
4. Acting with a partner—with and without words.
5. Emotion memory and sense memory.
6. Quarrel scenes—stage tension—building to the climax.
7. Elements of stage movement and grouping from the viewpoint of the Producer and actor—dressing the stage.
8. General crowd work and team playing.
9. Tempo, pace, rhythm.
10. Timing and the co-ordination of speech, gesture and movement.
11. The handling of properties.
12. Charged dialogue.
13. Scenes of mood.
14. Special requirements for comedy including farce and comedy of manners.
15. Special requirements for tragedy.
16. Special requirements for certain dramatists—
    Shakespeare
    Ibsen
    Chekhov
    Shaw
17. Characterisation—the approach to the role.
18. The actor and producer relationship—taking direction.
19. Theatre etiquette.
20. Preparation for auditions.

FIRST YEAR

FIRST TERM.

Exercises based on requirements of General Syllabus A. Nos.
1-6.

Set speeches.

Rehearsal of one-act play.

SECOND TERM.

Further exercises based on General Syllabus Nos. 7-12.

Crowd scenes rehearsed to performance standard.

Duologue scenes rehearsed and performed.

Rehearsal of a Play, e.g. *Time and the Conways*—Priestley.

THIRD TERM.

Continuation of rehearsals of the play chosen.

Preparation for the First Year Acting Test.

First Year Acting Test

1. One solo passage.
2. One duologue passage—the partners to be chosen by the
    instructor.

SECOND YEAR

FOURTH TERM.

General Syllabus, Nos. 13-20.

Rehearsal of representative scenes from

a. a comedy.

b. tragedy.

to dress rehearsal stage.

The emphasis to be on characterisation and team work.

The casting to be "against type" to enable students to extend
their range.

FIFTH TERM.

Revision of General Syllabus.

Rehearsal of entire acts of a Shakesperian Comedy and
Tragedy (or History).

Sɪxᴛʜ Tᴇʀᴍ.

Continuation of rehearsals of Shakesperian plays.

Preparation for the acting test.

Second Year Acting Test.

1. Set passages, e.g. Solo narrative.

2. Scene for 2/3 people.

3. Participation in a crowd scene.

4. Dialect passage.

THIRD YEAR

Sᴇᴠᴇɴᴛʜ Tᴇʀᴍ.

Preparation of as many contrasting roles as possible by students for performance and criticism in class.

Students given individual exercises according to their own needs.

Eɪɢʜᴛʜ ᴀɴᴅ Nɪɴᴛʜ Tᴇʀᴍs.

Rehearsal of two or more acts of plays to performance standard (or two or more one-act plays).

Lectures on play production and stage management.

A final lecture on theatre etiquette.

Assessment of progress of student during the course.

Note.

1. Voice and movement routines performed daily throughout the course. (See Chapters 12 and 13).

2. Dancing and Mime classes throughout the course.

3. Fencing introduced at beginning of fourth term.

APPENDIX II

List of Extracts from Plays

THIS list is intended to provide both student actor and teacher with additional material for practice in the aspects of acting technique discussed in this book. Each extract must be studied in relation to the play from which it is taken and rehearsed accordingly. The list can be extended as occasion demands.

AESCHYLUS

The Eumenides. Translated by Gilbert Murray.

> *Orestes:* I have known much evil, and have learnt therein
> What divers roads man goes to purge his sin . . .

JEAN ANOUILH

Ring Round the Moon. Translated by Christopher Fry.

> III ii. *Mme. Desmer:* He doesn't love you my dear, and
> he'll never love you.

BERTOLT BRECHT

The Good Woman of Setzuan. Translated by Eric Bentley.
Scene 10. Shen Te and the Gods.

> *Second God:* What did you do with our good woman of
> Setzuan?

ANTON CHEKHOV

The Seagull.

> I. *Treplev:* She loves me . . . she loves me not.

> III. Arcadina and Treplev.
> *Arcadina:* Sit down. You look as if you're wearing a
> turban.

The Cherry Orchard.

> II. *Trofimov:* All Russia is our orchard.

The Three Sisters.
I.   *Irina:* When I woke up this morning . . .
IV. *Olga:* How cheerfully that band's playing.

WILLIAM CONGREVE
The Way of the World.
IV. v. Millamant and Mirabell.
Mirabell: Have you any more conditions to offer?

NOEL COWARD
Still Life.
Laura: Loving you is hard for me.

GORDON DAVIOT
The Little Dry Thorn.
I. Abraham, Lot, Sarah and Milcah.
Lot: You are not worried about business, are you?

HENRIK IBSEN
The House of Rosmer. Translated by Brian J. Burton.
III. Rebecca and Rosmer.
Rosmer: What does this mean?
Rebecca: I'm going away.

DENIS JOHNSTON
The Moon in the Yellow River.
III. *Dobelle:* Well, I think that puts an end to my part . . .

BEN JONSON
The Alchemist.
The Prologue: Fortune, that favours fools . . .

NOEL LANGLEY
Little Lambs Eat Ivy.
II. Dougall and Essie.
Dougall: Essie. I've wanted to tell you something for a
long time.

CHRISTOPHER MARLOWE
Doctor Faustus.
　Chorus : Not marching in the fields of Thramisen . .
　V. ii. *Faustus:* O Faustus. Now hast thou but one bare
　　　　　hour to live.

W. SOMERSET MAUGHAM
The Letter.
　III. ii. *Leslie:* He came, and I told him I knew about the
　　　　　Chinawoman.

ARTHUR MILLER
The Crucible.
　IV. Proctor and Elizabeth.
　　Proctor:　The child?
　　Elizabeth: It grows.

JOHN MORTIMER
What Shall We Tell Caroline?
　Scene 2. Entrance and exit of Caroline.
　　Tony: She's going for a walk.

CLIFFORD ODETS
Waiting for Lefty.
　Agate: Ladies and Gentlemen, and don't let anyone tell you
　　　　we ain't got some ladies in this sea of upturned faces.
Awake and Sing.
　III. *Ralph:* Does it prove something?

LUIGI PIRANDELLO
Henry IV.
　II. *Henry:* Enough. Enough! Let's stop it.

J. B. PRIESTLEY
Dangerous Corner.
　III. *Olwen:* It's horrible to talk about.
Time and the Conways.
　III. *Carol:* Yes, I could of course, and I've often thought
　　　　about it.

BIBLIOGRAPHY

A short list of books which are recommended for further study.

Acting (General)

Barrault, Jean-Louis: *Reflections on the Theatre.* Translated by Barbara Wall. Macmillan.

Boleslavsky, Richard: *Acting.* Dobson.

Brecht, Bertolt: *Schriften zum Theater.* Suhrkamp Verlag. (Berlin and Frankfurt am Main).

Clurman, Harold: *The Fervent Years.* Dobson.

Coquelin, C: *The Art of the Actor.* Translated by Elsie Fogerty. Allen and Unwin.

Green, F. C. (Editor): *Diderot's Writings on the Theatre.* (in French). Cambridge University Press.

Jouvet, Louis: *Réflexions du comédien.* Editions du Sablon (Paris).

Rapoport, I: *The Work of the Actor.* Theatre Workshop. (New York).

Redgrave, Michael: *The Actor's Ways and Means.* Heinemann.
Mask or Face. Heinemann.

Stanislavsky, Constantin: *My Life in Art.* Translated by J. J. Robbins. Geoffrey Bles.
An Actor Prepares. Translated by Elizabeth Reynolds Hapgood. Geoffrey Bles.
Building a Character. (same translator). Reinhart and Evans.

White, Edwin: *Acting.* Herbert Jenkins.

Willett, John: *The Theatre of Bertolt Brecht.* Methuen.

Acting (Comedy)

Bergson, Henri: *Laughter*. Macmillan.

Lane, Lupino: *How to Become a Comedian*. Frederick Muller.

Seyler, Athene and
  Haggard, Stephen: *The Craft of Comedy*. J. Garnet Miller.

Movement and Mime

Battye, Marguerite: *Stage Movement*. Herbert Jenkins.

Mawer, Irene: *The Art of Mime*. Metheun.

Oxenford, Lyn: *Design in Movement*. J. Garnet Miller.
    Playing Period Plays. J. Garnet Miller.

Sayre, Gwenda: *Creative Miming*. Herbert Jenkins.

Speech Training

Bullard, Audrey, M: *Speech at Work*. Longmans.

Burniston, Christabel: *Speech in Practice*. English Speaking Board.

Coffin, L. Charteris: *Stage Speech*. Herbert Jenkins.

Thurburn, Gwynneth: *Voice and Speech*. Nisbet.

Turner, Clifford, J: *Voice and Speech in the Theatre*. Pitman.

School Drama

Burton, E. J: *Drama in Schools*. Herbert Jenkins.

Slade, Peter: *Child Drama*. University of London Press.

INDEX